PRE-INTERMEDIATE BUSINESS ENGLISH PRACTICE FILE

NEW EDITION

MARKET
LEADER

John Rogers

PEARSON
Longman

www.longman.com

FT
FINANCIAL

HARROW COLLEGE

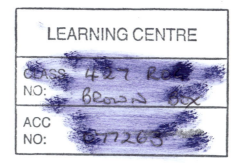

077263

Map of the Practice File

	Language work			Talk business	
	Vocabulary	**Language review**	**Writing**	**Sound work**	**Survival business English**
Unit 1 Careers page 4 / page 54	Words for talking about jobs	Ability Requests Past abilities	Past abilities Curriculum vitae Editing	**Individual sounds:** The difference between /ɪ/ and /iː/ **Connected speech:** *Can/Can't* **Stress and intonation:** Questions	Telephoning
Unit 2 Selling online page 8 / page 56	Words for talking about selling	Modals	Placing an order Replying to an order Editing	**Individual sounds:** Same or different **Connected speech:** *have to* **Stress and intonation:** Rising and falling intonation	Negotiating
Unit 3 Companies page 12 / page 58	Words for talking about companies	Present tenses	An informal e-mail Linkers	*-s* endings **Connected speech:** *are*	Company presentation
Unit 4 Great ideas page 16 / page 60	Words for talking about new ideas	Past tenses	Giving information Editing	*-ed* endings **Connected speech:** *was* and *were*	Meetings
Unit 5 Stress page 20 / page 62	Words for talking about stress in the workplace	The present perfect tense	Punctuation A report Editing	Groups of consonants **Connected speech:** *has/have*; *hasn't/haven't* **Stress and intonation:** Question tags	Making and responding to suggestions
Unit 6 Entertaining page 24 / page 64	Words for talking about food and drink	Multi-word verbs	A report A hotel booking	**Individual sounds:** The letter *a* **Connected speech:** Linking sounds	Making small talk

The sounds of English: page 52   **Sounds and spelling**: page 53   **Shadowing**: page 53

Careers

Vocabulary

A Complete the text with the best words.

> **Career advice for junior managers**
>
> Junior managers who ...... *b* ....¹ a promotion often face many problems when they have more authority and responsibility.
>
> This is partly because everyone expects them to perform to extremely high ....². In addition, many of their ....³ and colleagues are always ready to criticise any serious mistake they may ....⁴.
>
> What advice can we give to young managers, then? First of all, they should have ....⁵ in their own skills and abilities. If they are not sure that they can succeed, they are less likely to perform competently. They should also ....⁶ their progress regularly.
>
> Secondly, they should ....⁷ themselves ambitious goals so that through hard work and commitment to the company they can in fact ....⁸ them sooner than is expected of them.
>
> That is how they can ....⁹ both personal and professional success.

1	**a)** take	**b)** get	**c)** earn
2	**a)** level	**b)** standards	**c)** quality
3	**a)** superiors	**b)** secretaries	**c)** chefs
4	**a)** do	**b)** make	**c)** show
5	**a)** confidence	**b)** belief	**c)** strength
6	**a)** test	**b)** improve	**c)** evaluate
7	**a)** find	**b)** make	**c)** set
8	**a)** reach	**b)** move	**c)** work
9	**a)** achieve	**b)** grow	**c)** demand

B Complete the sentences with the appropriate form of an item from the box.

> ~~involve~~   be in charge   deal   look   make sure   be responsible

1 Marcel Lacour works for Research & Development. His job . *involves* ..... developing new products and new ideas.

2 Tatiana Vasilieva is the receptionist. She .... after visitors and takes messages.

3 Kate Hughes works for Administration and Personnel. She .... with staff problems, as well as with recruitment and training.

4 Linda Eriksen is our Quality Control Inspector. She .... for monitoring our products and trying to improve their quality.

5 Sergio Carboni is our new Maintenance Engineer. He checks all our equipment regularly and .... of all repairs.

6 Zoltan Jilly is our Security Officer. He .... that our staff and premises are protected against crime.

C Match these phrases from exercise B with the words that come immediately after them.

1 to be in charge   **a)** after
2 to deal   **b)** for
3 to look   **c)** that
4 to make sure   **d)** of
5 to be responsible   **e)** with

Language review
Requests

A Complete the interviewer's questions from a job interview with words from the box.

working	contact	let	moving	send	sharing	start

1 Would you mind ....*working*.... at weekends?
2 Could you .... us have your previous employer's details?
3 Would you mind .... our appointment to Monday?
4 Could you .... in two weeks' time?
5 Could you .... us as soon as possible?
6 Would you mind .... an office with three other people?
7 Could you .... us a copy of your certificates?

B Match the interviewee's answers to the interviewer's questions in exercise A.

a) Not at all, as long as it's in the morning. ☐ 3
b) Certainly. I'm free to start as soon as you like. ☐
c) Yes. I'll let you know my decision by Friday, if that's all right. ☐
d) Sure. I'll put copies in the post straightaway. ☐
e) That's fine, as long as it's a non-smoking area. ☐
f) How often would that be? ☐
g) Well, in fact they're all included in my CV. ☐

Past abilities

C Study the examples. Then complete the dialogues below with *could* or *was able to*.

Examples: • *could* (general ability)
                A: *Can you use a PC?*
                B: *Yes, I can. In fact, I <u>could</u> use a PC when I was 10!*
           • *was able to* (one occasion)
                A: *So were you late for the interview?*
                B: *No. Sue gave me a lift, so I <u>was able to</u> get there in time.*

1 A: What foreign languages can you speak?
   B: I .... speak Italian fluently at one time, but I've forgotten a lot.
2 A: What was your greatest achievement in your previous job?
   B: Well, I .... reorganise the Sales Department in a month.
3 A: What did you like best about your previous job?
   B: My boss really trusted me, so I .... use my own initiative.
4 A: So you worked in Turkey three years ago. Could you give us some details?
   B: Certainly. As a matter of fact, I .... win a very big contract.
5 A: So how did the interview go?
   B: Fine, I think. I .... answer all the questions!

Language work

**Writing
Curriculum
vitae**

 Complete Antonia's CV with the headings from the box.

| ~~Address~~ Achievements E-mail Experience Interests Personal details |
| Profile Qualifications Referees Special skills Telephone |

Curriculum vitae
Antonia Sophia Mehditash

1 .....Address.....   Rua Humberto Madeira 23, P – 3004-520
Coimbra, Portugal

2 ....   +351 239 856 207

3 ....   a.s.mehdi@netvisao.pt

4 ....

An Assistant Marketing Director in a medium-sized company, Orey Tours, seeking a more challenging position with more responsibility. Able to work on own initiative to tight deadlines.

5 ....

• Contributed to the development of a successful sales strategy
• Coordinated the work of the sales, marketing, and advertising personnel
• Designed Excel spreadsheets for sales records

6 ....

• Negotiating contracts with foreign and domestic airlines
• Working as part of team
• Proficient user of MS Windows, MS Word, MS Excel, Quark XPress

7 ....

2001–date   Assistant Marketing Director (Orey Tours, Coimbra)

July–Sept 2000   Work placement at Portugália Airlines (London office)

8 ....

1998–2000   MBA at Brentford College (UK / Distance course)

1994–1998   BA in Economics at the University of Coimbra

9 ....

Date of birth: 6 June 1975

Driving licence: Full, clean

10 ....

I sing in a choir and play basketball in an amateur team.

11 ....

Ana Luisa Santos
Professor of Economics
Avenida do Brasil 27
P – 1600 Lisboa
Tel: +351 1 722 0893
Email: alsantos@netcabo.pt

Ms Celia Gutlerner
Director MBA Programmes
Brentford College
27 Burrard Street
Brentford TW9 0AK
Email: mbadir@BMBA.ac.uk

B Put each item 1 – 5 under the appropriate heading in the CV in exercise A.

Heading number
8

1 1997: IELTS Certificate (Academic) – Overall Band 8

2 Designed Orey's website

3 Excellent conversational Spanish and some French

4 I enjoy helping other people design their websites.

5 An excellent team worker

C This draft letter of application is not appropriate. Rewrite it using some of the expressions from the Useful language box. Make any other necessary changes.

> Hello
>
> I saw your ad in our local paper last week, so I want to apply for the job of Communications Assistant. I know I am the person you're looking for. I just got various A-levels from school, and all my friends say they love chatting with me. So write soon, and tell me if you want to know more about me.
>
> Regards

Useful language

Dear Sir or Madam,

With reference to your advertisement in ...

I would like to apply for the position of ...

I feel I am well qualified for the position because ...

I would be happy to give you more details and can be contacted at any time.

Please let me know if there are any other details you need.

I enclose a copy of my CV.

A full CV is attached.

I look forward to hearing from you.

Yours faithfully,

Editing

D Read the text about how to prepare for a job interview.
- In each line 1 – 6 there is **one wrong word**.
- For each line, **underline the wrong word** in the text and **write the correct word** in the space provided.

Before you go for a job interview, make sure that you do your

homework. Find out as much as you <u>could</u> about the company, 1 can

about its history, about what it does, how many people it employ, 2 ....

and so on. During the interview, try to keeping to the point. Give 3 ....

complete answers, but do not talk for longer then necessary. 4 ....

Finally, remember that you can ask the interviewer question. This 5 ....

will show that you are really interested for the opportunity. 6 ....

Language work

Selling online

Vocabulary

A **Read the definitions. Then supply the missing vowels for each word.**

1 something you buy cheaply or for less than the usual price
2 a large building used for storing goods
3 to send goods to a place
4 a formal word meaning *to buy*
5 to give someone their money back (e.g., because they are not satisfied with what they have bought)

a b _ rg _ _ n
a w _ r _ h _ _ s _
to d _ sp _ tch
to p _ rch _ s _
to r _ f _ nd

B **Match each word to its definition.**

1 a supplier
2 a retailer
3 a wholesaler
4 an invoice
5 an order
6 turnover

a) a request by a customer for goods or services
b) a document sent by a seller to a customer that lists the goods sold and says how much they cost
c) a person or company that sells a particular type of product to a customer
d) the value of the goods or services sold during a certain period of time
e) a person or company that sells goods in large quantities to businesses
f) a company or a person that sells goods to members of the public

C **Complete each sentence with a word from exercise A or B.**

1 The machines were faulty, so we returned them to our ...*supplier*..... .
2 AlphaTex will place an .... on condition that we give them an extra discount for cash.
3 They guarantee that they will .... our money if we are not fully satisfied.
4 Our shop has a .... of 3,000 euros a week.
5 They promised to .... the goods within two days of our order, but they haven't arrived yet.

D **Complete the text with the best words from page 9.**

Selling online successfully

To be a successful online business, first of all you need to have a good website. A good website looks professional and is quick and easy to use. For instance, many people do not like to have to register to visit a site. It is also important for the company to have its ...*c*...1 on each page. This brands the site and can be used by the visitor as a link back to the ....2.

Of course, your products need to be at least as good as your site. The site may be what ....3 customers in the first place, but it is certainly the quality of the products and of the service that makes them come back. ....4 your prices down, and make a point of offering excellent after sales ....5.

Inform your visitors that you offer ....6 online ordering. Finally, when you receive an order, e-mail the customer to ....7 receipt and to inform them when the goods will be ....8.

1	a) flag	b) symbol	c) logo
2	a) homepage	b) modem	c) search engine
3	a) shows	b) appeals	c) attracts
4	a) Take	b) Give	c) Bring
5	a) service	b) guarantee	c) method
6	a) saved	b) proof	c) secure
7	a) thank	b) acknowledge	c) send
8	a) exchanged	b) despatched	c) purchased

Language review

Modals

A **Match each sentence to the meaning expressed by the modal in *italics*.**

1 Online retailers *should* offer secure online ordering.   ☐   **a)** It is not necessary.

2 You *have to* work very hard to attract visitors to your site.   ☐   **b)** It would be a good idea.

3 If you need a password, you *mustn't* let anyone else use it.   ☐   **c)** It is necessary.

4 People like it when they *don't have to* register to visit a site.   ☐   **d)** Don't do that!

B **Rewrite these sentences using an appropriate modal to replace the words in *italics*.**

1 If you want your website to be effective, *it is necessary to* work on it all the time.

   If you want your website to be effective, *you have to work on it all the time.*

2 *It is a good idea* for online retailers to despatch orders quickly.

   Online retailers ....

3 One of the good things about their website is that *it is not necessary to* register.

   One of the good things about their website is that you ....
   ....

4 *It is a good idea to* put your logo on every page of your site.

   You ....

5 If you order before 15 March, *it's not necessary* for you to pay until July.

   If you order before 15 March, you ....

6 This deal is very important for all of us, *so no mistakes please*!

   This deal is very important, so we .... !

C **Match the sentence halves.**

1 We were all in agreement,

2 You'll need your user ID and password each time,

3 We didn't have any more paper in stock,

4 We always order online,

5 If they have an online catalogue,

6 They say some of the goods are damaged,

a) so we had to order some more.

b) so we'll have to exchange them.

c) so we didn't need to discuss the deal any further.

d) which means we don't have to queue.

e) so you mustn't forget them.

f) we won't have to ask them to send us one.

D **Look at the sentence halves a) – f) in exercise C and complete the table.**

Past	Present	Future
....	*don't have to*	....
....	....	....

Language work

9

Writing
Placing an order

A Complete the online order form with the ten missing items.

a) 5   e) 155   i) Edinburgh
b) 10   f) 1,581.3   j) Unit price
c) 50   g) T-shirts
d) 83.20   h) Tim Atkinson

BEBOP TENNISGEAR ◆ SECURE ONLINE ORDER FORM ◆

Quantity	Item	Code	........j..........¹	Total cost
1	Ball machine	BM/709	€750	€750
.........²	'Champ' rackets	RCH43	€55	€550
50	'Tournament' balls	TB	€3.10	€.........³
.........⁴	'Regular' balls	RB	€2.49	€124.50
.........⁵	Gear bags	B27-H	€10	€50
10	.................⁶	T/12	€3.50	€35
			Gross total	€1,664.50
			Discount @ 5%	€.........⁷
			Net amount due	€.........⁸

Name: ....⁹

Company: Atkinson's Ultimate Sports Centre

Address: 45 Dalston Gardens

....¹⁰

Post code: EH5 5EY

Phone: 0131 548 8937

E-mail: atkinson@btinternet.com

THANK YOU!

Replying to an order

B Complete this formal e-mail with the appropriate form of an item from the box.

We look forward to doing / We would like to do   things /goods
Thanks / Thank you   All the best / Yours sincerely
Dear / Hello   Just to say / We confirm

To: atkinson@btinternet.com
Cc: bebopaccounts@easynet.co.uk
Subject: Your order 21/GT06

.... ¹ Mr Atkinson

.... ² for your order of 21 June.

.... ³ that you have ordered the following items from our online catalogue:

1	Ball machine	BM/709
10	'Champ' rackets	RCH43
50	'Tournament' balls	TB
50	'Regular' balls	RB
5	Gear bags	B27-H
10	T-shirts	T/12

Language work

We are now dealing with your order.

The sum of €1,581.30 has been charged to your credit card, and the .... ⁴ will be shipped on 24 June.

If you have any queries, please contact us at < bebopsales@easynet.co.uk>.

.... ⁵ business with you again.

.... ⁶

Neelum Singh

C The phrases below are often used when replying to an order. Complete them with words from the box.

| deliver | doing | hesitate | receipt | placing |

- Thank you for .... ¹ an order with (name of the company).
- Thank you for your order of (date).
- We confirm .... ² of your order dated ...

- Shipping normally takes two to three days/a week/etc.
- We can .... ³ within a week/a month/etc.

- Do not .... ⁴ to contact us if you need further information/further details.
- If you have any queries, please contact us.

- We look forward to further orders from you.
- Looking forward to .... ⁵ business with you again.

Editing **D** Read the text about writing business e-mails.
- In most of the lines **1 – 9** there is **one extra word** which does not fit. Some lines, however, are correct.
- If a line is **correct**, put a tick (✓) in the space provided.
- If there is an **extra word** in the line, write that word in the space.

Basically, the rules for writing business e-mails and letters are the same:	1	....✓........
be clear, be so polite, and do not write more than you have to. Over the	2	....so........
past ten years, business correspondence has generally become a simpler,	3	....
more informal – and this tendency is even more visible in e-mails. But	4	....
some things they have not changed. Clarity of layout is still important, so	5	....
you should to use paragraphs and space them out. Grammar and spelling	6	....
too need to be accurate and if you want to make a good impression on	7	....
your business partners. Even the best spellchecker cannot find all the	8	....
mistakes you make, so always to check your e-mails carefully.	9	....

Companies

Vocabulary

A Match the companies to the industry sector they belong to.

1 Apple, Dell, IBM, Microsoft
2 Nokia, Samsung, Siemens
3 Ikea, Tesco, Wal-Mart, Zara
4 AP Møller-Maersk, Qatar Airways, Ryanair, Virgin
5 BMW, General Motors, Nissan, Toyota
6 Deutsche Bank, HSBC, PricewaterhouseCoopers
7 Johnson & Johnson, Novartis

a) Healthcare
b) Financial
c) Transport
d) Retailing
e) IT (Information Technology)
f) Electrical / Electronics
g) Engineering

B Complete the extract from a company report with the best words.

ANNUAL REPORT   *ALFITEL*

Alfitel is committed to creating and delivering value — value to its customers, value to its employees and value to the region. Our success in moving towards this goal is most evident in the financial ....q.....[1] for this year. Our ....[2] at the close of the year was 140 million euros; that is an ....[3] of 12% over the previous year. This strong ....[4] in a rather difficult year for the economy shows the value of the service the company provides to its ....[5]. It also shows the commitment of its staff to this goal.

The pre-tax profit was 15.6 million euros, while the profit after tax was 8.8 million, which is 11% above that for the previous year.

I would like to congratulate our staff on their outstanding ....[6].

Finally, we all thank you, the ....[7], for your continuing support of the company.

1	**a)** results	**b)** conclusions	**c)** statistics
2	**a)** revenue	**b)** cash flow	**c)** share
3	**a)** asset	**b)** increase	**c)** advantage
4	**a)** trend	**b)** benefit	**c)** growth
5	**a)** customers	**b)** buyers	**c)** workforce
6	**a)** turnover	**b)** subsidiary	**c)** performance
7	**a)** producers	**b)** shareholders	**c)** stockbrokers

C Complete the names of the company departments in the definitions.

1 _ _s_ _ _ _h and _ _v_l_p_ _n_ is concerned with studying new ideas and planning new products.

2 _cc_ _ _ _s keeps a record of the money coming in and going out.

3 _dm_ _ _str_ _ _ _n is involved with managing and organising the work of a company.

4 H_ _ _n r_s_ _ _c_s deals with employees, keeps their records and helps with any problems they might have.

5 S_ _ _s and m_rk_ _ _ _g deals with selling and promoting its products.

Language review
Present tenses

A Match each sentence with the meaning expressed by the verb in *italics*.

1 TransChem *employs* 2,560 people.

2 Ms Dubois *is replacing* Phil as Sales Manager till October.

3 We *are improving* our services to meet the needs of a much wider range of customers.

4 We *are opening* our sixth subsidiary next month.

5 We *need* a different set of skills to address our company's challenges.

6 We *observe* our customers' reactions carefully.

a) temporary situation

b) future arrangement

c) ongoing situation

d) routine activity

e) factual information

f) verb usually used only in the present simple

B Correct the three sentences that use the wrong present tense.

1 Our company looks for a new Marketing Manager.

2 We rarely raise our prices by more than 3%.

3 We are bringing marketing and sales resources closer to customers.

4 Our largest subsidiary, based in Ottawa, is going through a difficult period.

5 This year, all our sales staff learn French.

6 At the moment, we are not knowing the profit figures.

C Complete the text with the correct form of verbs from the box. Use either the present simple or the present continuous tense.

coordinate attend go have know prepare speak think travel

Sofia Grammatopoulos is Marketing Manager at Kayavis Food & Wine S.A., an expanding medium-sized business in Thessaloniki. She *coordinates*.¹ the work of a team of three people. Kayavis ....² distributors in eleven countries in Europe and America, so Sofia often ....³ abroad. Next week, she ....⁴ to Canada to visit their new retail outlet. She ....⁵ Greek, English and Danish. At the moment she ....⁶ an intensive German course because the owner of Kayavis ....⁷ of opening a shop and a large restaurant in Munich. Sofia ....⁸ that she will have to work in Germany for six months, so she ....⁹ herself for her new assignment as best as she can.

D Make questions for these answers. All the information is in the text in exercise C.

1 *What does Sofia do?* She co-ordinates the work of a team of three people.

2 ....
Eleven.

3 ....
Next week.

4 ....
To visit their new retail outlet.

5 ....
Greek, English and Danish.

6 ....
Because she will have to work in Germany.

7 ....
In Munich.

Language work

13

Language work

Writing
An informal
e-mail

A Read the tip. Then put the lines of the informal e-mail in the correct order.

Tip

Remember that in business correspondence, information is often presented in the following order:
- appropriate greeting
- thanks and / or reference to previous contact
- main point
- other point(s)
- reference to future contact
- appropriate ending

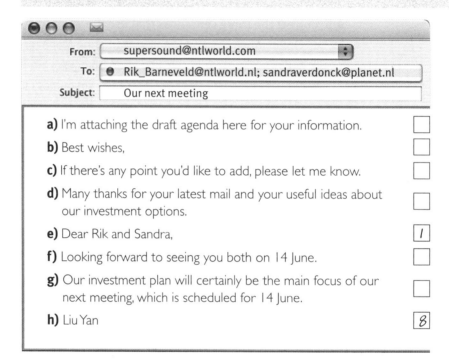

From: supersound@ntlworld.com

To: Rik_Barneveld@ntlworld.nl; sandraverdonck@planet.nl

Subject: Our next meeting

a) I'm attaching the draft agenda here for your information. ☐

b) Best wishes, ☐

c) If there's any point you'd like to add, please let me know. ☐

d) Many thanks for your latest mail and your useful ideas about our investment options. ☐

e) Dear Rik and Sandra, 1

f) Looking forward to seeing you both on 14 June. ☐

g) Our investment plan will certainly be the main focus of our next meeting, which is scheduled for 14 June. ☐

h) Liu Yan 8

B Write Rik's reply (50–70 words) to Liu's e-mail in exercise A.
- Include the points in the tip.
- In addition, suggest that *setting up online sales* should be on the agenda, and say *why*.

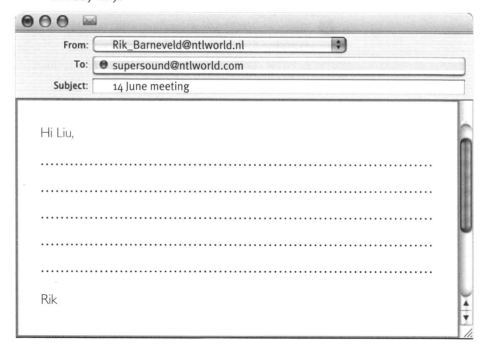

From: Rik_Barneveld@ntlworld.nl

To: supersound@ntlworld.com

Subject: 14 June meeting

Hi Liu,

....

....

....

....

....

Rik

C Read Sandra's reply to Liu's e-mail.

- In five of the lines **1 – 10** there is **one wrong word**.
  Five lines, however, are correct.
- If a line is **correct**, put a tick (✓) in the space provided.
- If there is a **wrong word** in the line, **underline the wrong word** in the text
  and write **the correct word** in the space provided.

From:	sandraverdonck@planet.nl
To:	● supersound@ntlworld.com
Subject:	14 June Meeting

Hello Liu,

Thanks you for informing me about the meeting, and for the agenda attached.	**1**	*Thank*
I am very sorry to tell you that, unfortunately, I won't be able to make 14th June	**2**	....✓.....
because of previous engagements. We have been looking for a new Office	**3**	....
Manager for our Utrecht subsidiary for almost a month, and we have now	**4**	....
shortlisted seven candidates. I'll be away 12th – 15th June to interview they, as	**5**	....
well as to sort out a couple of other matters related to the lease of our offices.	**6**	....
As I can't be there in person, I'm attach some ideas for the investment plan. I	**7**	....
hope they are of some use. I have also made some suggestion for the agenda.	**8**	....
Good luck with the meeting. I hope it goes as well as the April one!	**9**	....
Once again, please accept my apologise for not being there with you all.	**10**	....

Best wishes,

Sandra

Linkers

D Complete the sentences with the correct linker from the box.

because	but	so

1 It is a difficult time for the industry ....*but*....... our company is still growing.

2 The motivation of the sales staff is now increasing .... we bought some new company cars.

3 Sales are falling .... management does not seem very worried about it.

4 Sales were not as good as they had hoped .... they launched a marketing campaign.

5 The best option is to buy new machinery .... the old machines are always breaking down.

6 There is a steady growth in sales .... profits are not rising.

7 Local competition is extremely strong .... we are planning to buy out two local competitors.

8 We are planning to open a new store in New York next year .... we want a foothold in the US market.

9 We increased our market share considerably, ... our share price rose to an all-time high.

10 We were unable to finance the new project .... of severe cash flow problems.

4 Great ideas

Vocabulary

A Match the verbs and nouns.

Verbs	Nouns
1 to hold	a) a business idea
2 to make	b) the environment
3 to reduce	c) a meeting
4 to address	d) money
5 to protect	e) a need
6 to develop	f) waste

B Use the correct form of a verb–noun combination from exercise A to complete the sentences.

1 The marketing department *held a meeting* last week to discuss their new strategy.

2 Eco-consumers choose companies which do not produce a lot of toxic waste and have a clear policy of ....

3 A good business idea is one that generates profits and at the same time ....

4 Brainstorming is an effective way of ....

5 Industrialised countries should try to .... instead of exporting it, as they often do.

6 With his Million Dollar Homepage, Alex Tew .... very quickly.

C Complete the text with the best words from page 17.

The way of the wiki

In the Hawaiian language, *wiki* means 'quick'.

Wikipedia was ...*c*... [1] by Jimmy Wales and Larry Sanger as a free online encyclopedia written by anybody who wants to contribute. Wales and Sanger were already working on an encyclopedia when in January 2001 they .... [2] the Wikipedia website. The greatest .... [3] was that any of its users could add or edit articles. At the beginning some academics criticised Wikipedia. They said it had a number of inaccuracies and therefore refused to recognise it as a reference work. But its extraordinary success showed that it was certainly good enough to .... [4] the needs of millions of users. It may not be a true business idea because it probably does not make a lot of .... [5], but it is certainly an idea that fills a .... [6] in the market.

Wikipedia's extraordinary .... [7] shows that lots of basic information can be exchanged by people who know things because of where they live, their hobbies or their education.

Today, Wikipedia is active in about 100 languages, and its English-language edition has more than half a million .... [8] about an enormous .... [9] of subjects.

1 **a)** worked   **b)** achieved   **c)** developed
2 **a)** launched   **b)** extended   **c)** solved
3 **a)** creation   **b)** innovation   **c)** trend
4 **a)** meet   **b)** respond   **c)** fill
5 **a)** benefit   **b)** turnover   **c)** money
6 **a)** hole   **b)** gap   **c)** demand
7 **a)** raise   **b)** growth   **c)** supply
8 **a)** articles   **b)** notices   **c)** texts
9 **a)** sort   **b)** award   **c)** range

Language review
Past tenses

A Match the sentence halves.

1 They were still working on their new designs

2 As they had an exciting idea to promote,

3 High-profile entrepreneurs were invited on TV

4 In 1985, Nicholas Albery founded

5 Albery learned not only how to produce new ideas

6 She was exhibiting at the Inventors' Fair

a) when a Korean entrepreneur expressed interest in her new product.

b) but also tested them in his daily life.

c) when they saw an opening in the market.

d) they decided to exhibit at the Inventors' Fair.

e) and asked to talk about innovation and change.

f) the Institute for Social Inventions.

B Rewrite the sentences which use the wrong past tense.

1 Hiltex was immediately filing patents for its new machines as it was worried that its competitors would copy them.
Hiltex immediately filed patents for its new machines as it was worried that its competitors would copy them.

2 Z40, the new drug developed by Pharmatek, marked a breakthrough in the treatment of cancer.

3 Their competitors failed to see the gap in the market and so missed a great opportunity.

4 At first, the agency was not believing that the machine would save so much time.

5 Zirkon already made good profits when it introduced its new digital camera in 2000.

6 The story goes that he was having the idea for the electric shoebrush while he was washing up.

7 I was planning to visit the International Inventors' Fair, but I did not have time.

C Put the verbs in brackets in the correct tense, past simple or past continuous.

1 Our company .was losing. [a] (*lose*) money at an alarming rate, but then in 2004 we . . . . [b] (*launch*) our Hermes MP3 player. Sales . . . . [c] (*rocket*), and our financial situation . . . . [d] (*improve*) rapidly.

2 She . . . . [e] (*decide*) to take a few months off in 1999, when she . . . . [f] (*work*) for Clairval Cosmetics. While she . . . . [g] (*tour*) New Zealand, she . . . . [h] (*develop*) an interest in Maori culture. She . . . . [i] (*take*) samples of some of the plants used in their rituals because she . . . . [j] (*believe*) they could be used in some of her company's products.

3 We . . . . [k] (*plan*) to patent our new drug, but we . . . . [l] (*wait*) far too long. A month after our discovery, our main competitor . . . . [m] (*sell*) basically the same product.

Writing
Giving information

A Put the lines of the message in the correct order.

MESSAGE:

a) *I want to take our 15 Spanish visitors* ☐ *1*

b) *as they are leaving early Monday morning.* ☐

c) *of the Spanish version of the catalogue.* ☐

d) *opening hours, entrance fee and price* ☐

e) *Please find out the following for me:* ☐

f) *to the Exhibition of Inventions on Sunday,* ☐

B Write a reply, based on the following information.

INTERNATIONAL EXHIBITION OF INVENTIONS, NEW TECHNIQUES AND PRODUCTS

Geneva:

PALEXPO

1st–5th May

Useful Information

Dates: 1st–5th May

Place: Palexpo – Geneva

Opening hours: 10am to 7pm

Sunday: 10am to 6pm

Admission charge: Fr12.00

Tickets available at the doors of the exhibition.

Children under the age of 15: Fr8.00

Groups of 10 or more: Fr8.00 per person

Official catalogue: Contains a description of all the inventions (available in French and English only): Fr25.00

Hotel reservation: Central Tourist Office
P.O. Box 1649–CH–1244 Genève 1
Tel. 00 4122 908 73 24   Fax 00 4122 908 73 25

Please contact your nearest travel agent for special rates.
Quote the name of the event and the code IDS 39K.

MESSAGE:

On Sunday, the International
Exhibition is open from

....

C You work for a large insurance company which always has large quantities of confidential documents to destroy. At the Exhibition of Inventions, you saw a new type of shredder.

Write an e-mail (75–85 words) to your Head of Department, including:

- some details about the machine, e.g., shreds paper and cardboard / fully automatic / fitted with energy-saving device / very quiet, etc.
- why you think it would be a good idea to buy this machine
- where your Head of Department might get further information.

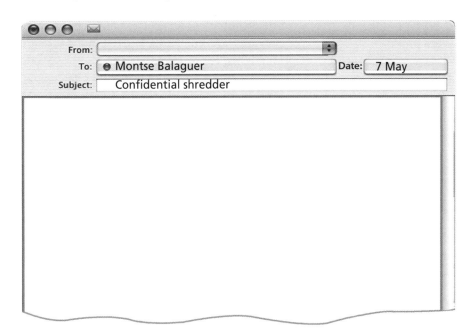

From:

To: ● Montse Balaguer   Date: 7 May

Subject: Confidential shredder

Language work

Editing **D** **Read the text about Jeff Bezos, the founder of Amazon.**

- In seven of the lines **1 – 10** there is **one extra word** which does not fit. Three lines, however, are correct.
- If a line is **correct**, put a tick (✓) in the space provided.
- If there is an **extra word** in the line, write that word in the space.

Jeff Bezos was just 31 when he launched Amazon.com in 1995. The road to	1 ....✓......
success was long and hard, but his company later it became the internet's biggest	2 ...*it*......
retailer, with the revenues of almost $2bn and a customer base of over 10 million.	3 ....
To his fans, Bezos is a visionary, a retail revolutionary in the tradition of Richard	4 ....
Sears, whose mail-order business was changed American shopping in the late	5 ....
19th and early 20th centuries. 'He saw the future in a concrete way before they	6 ....
anyone else did,' says Brad Silverberg, co-founder of a Seattle-based and venture	7 ....
capital firm. 'He has done more than anyone else never in the world to change	8 ....
everyone's buying habits. People go to the web and buy stuff because of Jeff	9 ....
Bezos. He created a household word – that's for an amazing accomplishment.' To	10 ....

many, Bezos will always remain the man who taught the world to shop online.

Stress

Vocabulary

A **Complete the text with the best words.**

The dictionary defines stress as 'a continuous feeling of worry that prevents you from relaxing'. At work, there are a lot of potentially stressful situations. For example, having to ...*c*...[1] a formal meeting or to ....[2] a presentation to senior executives can cause stress, especially the first time. In fact, all kinds of situations are more stressful when you have never found yourself in them before.

However, experience does not always solve the problem. Indeed, many people say that they always feel under stress when ....[3] a valuable contract or meeting important visitors from abroad, or even just when working to ....[4] deadlines. Other situations that employees generally find difficult to cope with include dealing with a customer who has a ....[5], or asking the boss for a pay ....[6].

All the situations mentioned above are examples of short-term stress. Experts agree that this kind of stress is less damaging to health than long-term stress, which happens when employees constantly work ....[7] pressure or have to cope with an ever-increasing ....[8]. In such cases, a complete change of ....[9] can of course be a solution, but companies should try to reduce stress levels before their employees are severely ....[10]. Otherwise, absenteeism may increase, and some staff may even decide to ....[11].

1 a) direct	**b)** go	**c)** lead
2 a) make	**b)** speak	**c)** show
3 a) dealing	**b)** negotiating	**c)** transferring
4 a) sharp	**b)** tight	**c)** narrow
5 a) complaint	**b)** complaining	**c)** complain
6 a) rising	**b)** bargain	**c)** rise
7 a) on	**b)** in	**c)** under
8 a) workload	**b)** workforce	**c)** workaholic
9 a) life cycle	**b)** lifetime	**c)** lifestyle
10 a) worked out	**b)** overworked	**c)** worked over
11 a) recruit	**b)** resign	**c)** participate

B **Complete the sentences with the correct prepositions from the box.**

in	of	to

1 Being stuck ..*in*.... a traffic jam on your way .... work can be quite stressful, especially if you have an important appointment.

2 Dat@ready is part .... a multinational company based .... Rotterdam.

3 As a result .... the merger, the management cut the workforce by 10%.

4 .... her report, the consultant notes that there has been a significant increase .... stress levels .... all departments .... our company .... the last eight months.

5   Our staff need a manager they can talk .... , not just someone who controls them.

6   He says going .... a stress counsellor is out .... the question.

7   I wish I could relax a bit more instead .... having to work .... strict deadlines all the time.

Language review

The present perfect tense

A **Four business people were asked about stressful experiences. Look at the table; then answer the questions, as in the examples.**

	Have you ever asked your boss for a pay rise?	Have you ever made a formal presentation?	Have you ever negotiated an important contract?
Sergio	✗	✓	✗
Marie	✓	✗	✓
Lucy	✓	✗	✗

1   Has Sergio ever made a formal presentation? *Yes, he has* .

2   Has Sergio ever asked his boss for a pay rise? *No, he hasn't* .

3   Has Marie ever negotiated an important contract? ....

4   Has Marie ever made a formal presentation? ....

5   Have Lucy and Sergio ever negotiated an important contract? ....

6   Have Lucy and Marie ever asked their boss for a pay rise? ....

7   Has anybody ever made a formal presentation? ....

B **Now read about other people's stressful experiences, and make questions for the answers.**

	Been late for an important meeting	Dealt with an aggressive customer	Suffered from jet-lag
Tim	✔	✗	✗
Paola	✗	✔	✗
Mark	✔	✔	✗

1   *Has Paola ever been late for an important meeting?* ....   **a)** No, she hasn't.

2   *Have Tim and Mark ever been late for an important meeting?*   **b)** Yes, they have.

3   ....   **c)** Yes, she has.

4   ....   **d)** No, he hasn't.

5   ....   **e)** No, they haven't.

6   ....   **f)** No, she hasn't.

C **Complete the text with the correct form (past simple or present perfect) of the verbs in brackets.**

"I *'ve worked* .... [1] (work) for Dat@ready since last summer. So far it .... [2] (be) enjoyable and I .... [3] (not /have) any difficulties. At the beginning I .... [4] (expect) to have a lot of problems, though. I .... [5] (think) I might not get on with my colleagues, but all of them .... [6] (be) friendly and supportive since the very first day. Last week, for example, I .... [7] (have to) meet some tight deadlines, which .... [8] (be) quite stressful. One of my colleagues .... [9] (offer) to collect all the data I .... [10] (need) for the quarterly report. This .... [11] (save) me at least half a day's work. I .... [12] (work) in four different countries over the last ten years, but I .... [13] (never / feel) so welcome as at Dat@ready, I must say."

Language work

Writing
Punctuation

A **Rewrite the paragraph, using punctuation and capital letters where necessary.**

according to a recent survey over 14% of all employed people in the eu suffer from stress two of the main reasons are overwork and fear of redundancies in addition a large number of employees are suffering from headaches backache and chest pains because of overcrowded offices poor ventilation and badly designed furniture and equipment over the last few years this has resulted in increased levels of absenteeism and a gradual decrease in productivity

B **Put the word groups in the correct order to make two sentences, a) and b), in each of the four sections.**

1 **a)** at some point / / in their life. / stress / Everyone experiences
   b) handle stress / But men and / very differently. / women generally
   Everyone experiences stress at some point in their life.
   But men and women generally handle stress very differently.

2 **a)** from stress-related illnesses. / women suffer / However, more / men than /
   b) as good / coping strategies / as women's. / That is / are not / because their

3 **a)** come from / from work. / home and / These pressures
   b) are only / at work. / many men / under pressure / By contrast,

4 **a)** are much / than men. / To begin / more flexible / with, women
   b) with the / Also, they / than men. / pressures better / usually cope

C **Put the four sections in exercise B in the best possible order (a–d) to make a paragraph.**

a) ..!.. 　　b) ..... 　　c) ..... 　　d) .....

A report

D **Write a report for the International Health Symposium based on the graph.**

1 Complete sentences **a) – f)** with the correct form (present simple, past simple or present perfect) of the verbs in brackets.

2 Put the sentences in the right order.

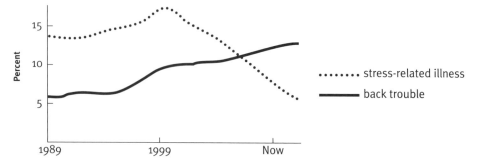

a) The graph ..shows..[1] (*show*) the changes in the percentage of the workforce staying off work because of back trouble and stress-related illness. ☐ *I*

b) Secondly, absences caused by stress-related illness ....[2] (*show*) a similar trend in the period 1989–1999. They ....[3] (*increase*) by 3%, to reach 17% in 1999. ☐

c) In conclusion, back trouble is still a problem today, but we ....[4] (*make*) excellent progress in bringing down the percentage of the workforce absent from work because of stress. ☐

d) To begin with, we can see that absences caused by back trouble ....[5] (*rise*) gradually since 1989. ☐

e) Since 1999, however, they .... [6] (*fall*) dramatically and now .... [7] (*stand*) at 7%.

f) Their percentage .... [8] (*go up*) from 6% in 1989 to 11% ten years later, and it now .... [9] (*stand*) at about 13%.

Useful language

The graph / table / slide shows ...
As you can see on this graph / table / slide ...

Firstly, ...
To begin with, ...

Secondly, ...
Next, ...

Finally, ...

To conclude, ...
In conclusion, ...

E Your boss, Daniel Duval, wanted you to take part in an important seminar tomorrow morning. You cannot go because you have a terrible headache. In fact, you have not slept very well for a week.
Write a message (60–80 words) to your boss.

- Apologise and say why you cannot attend.
- Tell him what you plan to do about your health.

MESSAGE

To: *Daniel Duval*
From:

Editing

F Read the text about stress at work.

- In each line **1 – 6** there is **one wrong word**.
- For each line, **underline the wrong word** in the text and **write the correct word** in the space provided.

Reducing stress is in the interest of both employers and employees.

First of all, less stress <u>mean</u> more productivity because, as everybody knows, the   **1** .*means*.

results of stress are often illness and absent from work. Every year, millions   **2** ....

of days of work is lost because of stress and stress-related illness.   **3** ....

As regards employees, on the other hand, a lower level of stress leading not only to   **4** ....

increased job satisfaction, but also to best relationships at work and at home. Of   **5** ....

course, it also contributes a great deal to a generally feeling of happiness.   **6** ....

Entertaining

Language work

Vocabulary

A Complete the story with the words from the box.

~~book~~ aperitif bill course delicious dessert dishes abroad
guest manager menu negotiate order starter stressful wide

I had chosen 'The Three Swans' because everybody said it was one of the best restaurants in town, but I had never been there myself. It was quite busy when we arrived. Fortunately, I had asked my secretary to ...*book*..... ¹ a table in advance. From where we were seated, we had a stunning view across the lake. My .... ², Mr Doulos, seemed quite pleased. Entertaining an important visitor from .... ³ was always a bit .... ⁴, but now I began to relax. I suggested having an .... ⁵, but Mr Doulos said he hardly ever drank alcohol, and certainly never on working days. I hoped I hadn't made a gaffe! We looked at the lunch .... ⁶, which was quite varied. There was a .... ⁷ variety of typical .... ⁸ from our region, and each one was described in a few words. When the waiter came to take our .... ⁹, Mr Doulos surprised me once more. He had chosen stuffed peppers as a .... ¹⁰, but he wanted to have them served *after* the main .... ¹¹. 'This is not a funny custom from my country,' he said with a smile. 'Just a personal preference.' The food was absolutely .... ¹². We talked only briefly about the contract we had to .... ¹³ that afternoon.

As it was getting late, we didn't have a .... ¹⁴, just coffee, and then I asked for the .... ¹⁵. But when I reached for my wallet, I realised to my horror that I didn't have it with me. Of course – it was at home, in my other jacket. No cash or credit card – how embarrassing! The only solution I could think of was to ask the manager to call MCI, my company. 'MCI? Is that Micro Computers International?' the manager asked. Indeed it was. 'No need to phone, sir; we'll put this on your account,' the manager continued. 'MCI has had an account with us for three years. And my wife is MCI's marketing .... ¹⁶.' Mr Doulos and I looked at each other, and we both burst out laughing. The day was saved.

B Complete each sentence with the best word.

1 Many people have only two .... a day: breakfast and dinner.
   a) meals **b)** dishes **c)** courses

2 Jane invited me round for dinner last night. Her husband is a wonderful ....
   a) cooker **b)** dish **c)** cook

3 Tom worked in Bangkok for a year, so he is very keen on Thai ....
   a) kitchen **b)** cooking **c)** cuisine

4 They are vegetarians, so we should not buy any ....
  a) meal   **b)** meat   **c)** food

5 This chocolate mousse is delicious. Could I have the ....?
  a) recipe   **b)** cookbook   **c)** receipt

Language review
Multi-word verbs

A Match the sentence halves.

1 Last week, I had to look
2 First, I showed them around
3 I certainly look forward
4 I hope I can take
5 One of them did not turn
6 The food was delicious, and we all got
7 Then, I took them
8 They said I should

a) come over and see them in Coimbra.
b) the Old Town.
c) after five clients from Portugal.
d) on really well.
e) out to a very good restaurant.
f) to seeing them all again.
g) up their invitation next summer.
h) up, unfortunately.

B Put the sentences from exercise A in the right order to make a story.

a) ..1.. b) ..5.. c) ...... d) ...... e) ...... f) ...... g) ...... h) ......

C Correct the wrong particle in two of the sentences.

1 Our manager is always looking out for new ways to entertain our clients.
2 They had to put off the meeting because too many employees were off sick.
3 Our visitors will be disappointed if nobody turns in at the airport to meet them.
4 The party we held for our Australian guests set us back €8,000.
5 I hope our colleagues will come around with some suggestions for the reception.

D Replace the phrases in *italics* with the correct form of a multi-word verb from the box.

| ~~work out~~ set up shop about slow down |
| set aside stand up for look for |

1 We *have developed* an action plan to reduce stress in our department.
  have worked out

2 The doctor said I was overworked and advised me to *become less active*.
  ....

3 You have to respect your superiors, of course, but you also have to *defend your opinions*.
  ....

4 We *tried to find* a new Sales Manager with at least three years' experience.
  ....

5 If you want to buy a new computer, it is a good idea to *go to different places to compare prices*.
  ....

6 At the time, the government was trying to encourage people to *start* new businesses.
  ....

7 The company's owners *have kept* €500,000 *so that this money is available later* to invest in their business.
  ....

Language work

Writing
A report

A Two thousand executives from different countries named their three favourite forms of entertainment when they are abroad on business.
- Look at the bar chart showing the results of the survey.
- Then complete the report with the phrases from the box.

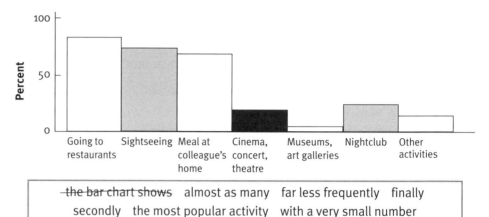

~~the bar chart shows~~ almost as many   far less frequently   finally
secondly   the most popular activity   with a very small number

.*The bar chart shows*.¹ how popular certain forms of entertainment are with executives while they are abroad on business. ....²
is clearly going to restaurants: 85% of the executives interviewed mentioned it in their top three. ....³ , seeing the sights was mentioned by 75% of the respondents, and ....⁴ said they enjoyed being invited round to a colleague's home for a meal.

Other forms of entertainment were mentioned ....⁵.
About 25% of the respondents enjoy going to a nightclub, and 20% to the cinema, the theatre or a concert. Museums and art galleries are popular ....
...................................⁶ of executives: only about 5%.
........................⁷ , other activities such as playing tennis, guided tours, wine or beer tasting, etc. were mentioned by 15% of the respondents.

A hotel booking

B Your company is organising a one-day conference on Friday 6th June. You are expecting delegates from your overseas branches.
Match the sentence halves in this e-mail from the Canadian branch.

From: Jim.Byrne@lycos.com
To: BMarks@easynet.co.uk
Subject:

1 Could you book one single room
2 If possible, he would prefer
3 He's arriving on Thursday 5th
4 Don't book him into the Royal this time,
5 Could you find him somewhere comfortable,

a) and leaving on the 7th in the morning
b) but not too expensive?
c) a non-smoking room.
d) in the name of Robert Dorey.
e) as it's too far from the centre.

Thanks.

Jim

C Look at the advertisement. Then reply to the e-mail in exercise B in 30–40 words, confirming the booking and giving some details about the hotel.

Astoria Hotel
☆ ☆ ☆

Double rooms from £150.00
Single rooms from £100.00
Prices include English or Continental Breakfast
Non-smoking 4th and 5th floor
Just a 5-minute walk from the city centre
The best value for money!

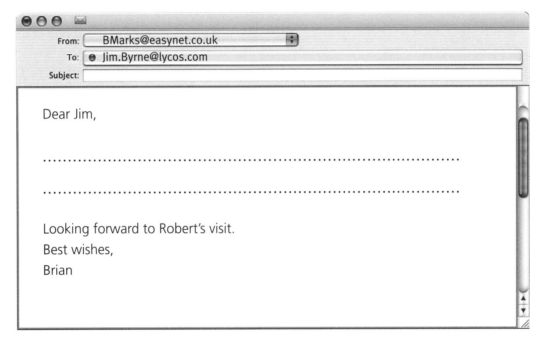

From: BMarks@easynet.co.uk
To: Jim.Byrne@lycos.com
Subject:

Dear Jim,

....

....

Looking forward to Robert's visit.
Best wishes,
Brian

D Rewrite Robert's e-mail, using paragraphs, punctuation and capital letters where necessary.

From: robdorey@lycos.com
To: BMarks@easynet.co.uk
Subject:

dear brian this is to thank you for your hospitality during and after the conference you gave me a lot of your time and made my visit very memorable walking round the old town in the evening was really fascinating besides i thought the food in that mediterranean restaurant where we had supper was just perfect it was a great pleasure to meet you if you come to canada i would like to return your kindness and generosity once again thank you regards robert

Marketing

Vocabulary

A Use the clues to complete the crossword puzzle.

Across

1 The percentage of sales a company or a product has is its market .... (5)

5 Companies sometimes promote their products by giving ...... gifts to customers. (4)

6 Companies carry out market research to get information about what buyers ...... and want. (4)

7 The life ...... of a product is the length of time people continue to buy it. (5)

9 An advertising campaign takes place over a period of time and usually has a specific .... (3)

10 Good marketing should increase the volume of .... (5)

11 A company's sales target is how much it wants to ...... in a certain period of time. (4)

Down

2 An advertising ...... advises companies on advertising. (6)

3 A company's product ...... is a set of products made by that particular company. (5)

4 A company's advertising ...... is the amount of money available for advertising during a particular period. (6)

5 Sales ...... show how much a company has sold over a certain period of time. (7)

8 Production ...... are what a company must spend on production. (5)

9 Besides giving advice to companies, an advertising agency can also make .... for them. (3)

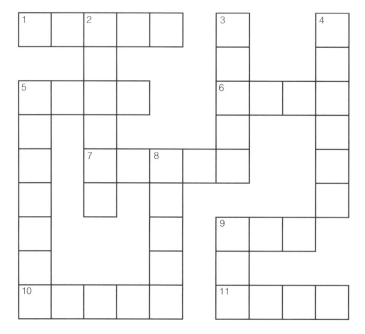

B Complete the text with the best words.

THE NAME GAME

A brand can be defined as a name given to a product by a company so that the product can easily be recognised by its name or its design. In our very ...*b*.... [1] business world, a good brand is one of the keys to the success of any company. It is often a powerful .... [2] tool.

However, the name is not everything. For a brand to be successful, marketers have to know what the consumer .... [3] and wants, so a lot of market .... [4] is necessary. This gives them a 'consumer .... [5], that is to say a kind of picture of the typical customer. It is a picture not only of the customer's needs and wants, but also of their beliefs and values. If the brand then clearly reflects those values, it is more likely to be successful.

The customer has so much .... [6] nowadays that a good brand is a necessity, so that one product is clearly different from another in his or her mind.

A good brand of course has long-term benefits, as it will .... [7] to many different market .... [8] and to people from different cultures.

1	**a)** informative	**b)** competitive	**c)** conservative
2	**a)** sales	**b)** sell	**c)** sold
3	**a)** wishes	**b)** needs	**c)** orders
4	**a)** study	**b)** research	**c)** science
5	**a)** summary	**b)** report	**c)** profile
6	**a)** choice	**b)** option	**c)** suggestion
7	**a)** attract	**b)** persuade	**c)** appeal
8	**a)** shares	**b)** portions	**c)** segments

Language review
Asking questions

A Complete the questions with words from the box.

> when   how long   how many   how much   what   which   who   why

1 ...*When*....... did you launch this advertising campaign?
2 .... didn't you contact an advertising agency?
3 .... money did you spend on the campaign?
4 .... new products did you launch? Was it two or three?
5 .... did you target your new product at?
6 .... market segments has your product been most successful in?
7 .... do you expect people to continue to buy this product?
8 .... is your sales forecast?

B Match the Marketing Manager's responses (a – h) to the interviewer's questions in exercise A.

a) Almost 20,000 euros.   [3]

b) As I said, it's been doing extremely well, and we expect a considerable increase in winter.   ☐

c) In late spring.   ☐

d) So far it's been doing very well with middle-class males in their thirties to mid-fifties.   ☐

e) We had health-conscious people in mind, as well as the elderly.   ☐

f) We think it will have a life cycle of about three years.   ☐

g) Well, we like to rely on our own people.   ☐

h) This time only one, in fact. But it is a very special product indeed.   ☐

C Put the words in the questions in the correct order.

1 mean/does/What/'launch'/?
What does 'launch' mean?

2 like/Manager/our/talk/you/to/to/Would/Marketing/?

3 a/advertising/Do/lot/on/spend/they/?

4 advertise/did/range/their/they/Where/new/?

5 targets/meet/Did/your/you/sales/?

6 expecting/figures/sales/Were/better/you/?

7 my/Have/sales/read/report/you/quarterly/?

8 a/How/do/often/report/write/you/?

D Match the answers a)–h) to the questions in exercise C.

a) Not yet, I'm afraid. I'll go through it first thing this afternoon. [7]

b) Well, they do have a large budget, yes. ☐

c) Every quarter. In the past we had to write one every month, though. ☐

d) To make a new product available to the public. ☐

e) Yes, that would be very useful. Thank you. ☐

f) In all national papers, and also on TV. ☐

g) No, we are very satisfied. In fact, we've sold a lot more than we thought. ☐

h) We certainly did. ☐

Writing

Answering an enquiry

A You work for the Marketing Department of Hamilton Food and Drink Products. You receive the following enquiry. Write a reply based on the notes below.

Dear Sir,

I am interested in your range of diet products, which I saw advertised in *Healthy Home*.

Could you please send me a copy of your catalogue? Further details of your new brand of mineral water would also be very welcome.

Many thanks.

Wim Rijsbergen

Notes

thanks for enquiry / enclose catalogue / also enclose leaflet about Fontaine, your latest brand of spring water + say a few words about this product (offers real benefits; recommended by medical authorities) / offer to send representative with sample / end suitably

Reports

B Put the following sentences from a report in the correct order (1 – 7). The words in bold will help you.

a) About one fifth of the consumers who have tried **our new products** said they were dissatisfied with the taste of the *Spring Balm* toothpaste. Also, 47 people complained of skin irritation after using our deodorant spray. ☐

b) **I shall begin with** my findings about the products themselves. ☐

c) **It** is based on information gathered from over 500 interviews with consumers. ☐

d) **On the other hand,** many of those who *have* heard about the *Spring Balm* collection complain that they cannot find our products anywhere. 7

e) **Secondly,** as regards the price, almost 90% remarked that our products are overpriced in comparison with well-established brands. ☐

f) **The aim of this report** is to determine the reasons for the failure of the launch of our new range of *Spring Balm* toiletries. 1

g) **Thirdly,** with regard to promotion and place, it is clear that the name *Spring Balm* still means nothing to most consumers. ☐

C Now complete the Recommendations section of the report with words from the box.

~~basis~~ available delay regard retail sure withdrawn

On the ...*basis*.....¹ of the above findings, I would like to make the following recommendations.

I recommend that the deodorant spray should be temporarily ....² and submitted to laboratory tests without ....³. Our laboratory should also develop a new flavour for the toothpaste.

With ....⁴ to price, we should look carefully at our competitors' policy and make ....⁵ that our price is correct.

Finally, I suggest that we should advertise more on TV and possibly on the Internet, and make sure that the *Spring Balm* collection is ....⁶ not only from a wider range of supermarkets, but also from more specialised ....⁷ outlets.

Editing

D Read the text about the Museum of Brands.

- In most of the lines **1 – 10** there is **one extra word** which does not fit. Some lines, however, are correct.
- If a line is **correct**, put a tick (✓) in the space provided.
- If there is **an extra word** in the line, write that word in the space.

The role of branding and advertising in a modern life has been put into historical	1 ....a.........
context at a new museum in London.	2 .....✓.........
The Museum of Brands, Packaging and Advertising will shows 200 years of	3 ....
consumer history and has displays of thousands of the brands and products.	4 ....
Robert Opie, the museum's director, he started the collection at the age of 16. It	5 ....
now includes all aspects of daily life – toys, comics, magazines and fashion. Mr	6 ....
Opie hopes the museum will it develop into a resource for marketing professionals	7 ....
who want to understand how today's companies sold themselves and in the past.	8 ....
The organisers say that the museum will 'reflect how daily life has changed with	9 ....
the arrival of numerous new brands, from milk on chocolate and cornflakes to	10 ....
yoghurt and soft margarine'. **FINANCIAL TIMES**	

Planning

Vocabulary

A Cross out the noun which does not normally combine with the verb in the bubble.

1

to estimate

costs
a price
the value of something
~~a report~~

2

to forecast

sales
a profit
a schedule
an increase

3

to plan

a meeting
information
a trip
a conference

4

to do

a profit
research
business
a lot of work

B Cross out the verb which does not normally combine with the noun in the bubble.

1

to draw up
~~to call~~
to overspend
to stick to

a budget

2

to decrease
to stick to
to implement
to evaluate

a plan

3

to cancel
to implement
to arrange
to reschedule

a meeting

4

to finish
to submit
to keep within
to write

a report

C Complete each sentence with a word combination from exercise A or B.

1 Experts ..._estimate_.. the ...._value_.... of the deal at 20 million euros.
2 We have to .... the .... for Friday because the CEO is busy all day Thursday.
3 My boss is angry because I haven't quite .... my sales .... yet, and she expected it last week.
4 We always .... on our products, so we can prove that they are the safest on the market.
5 Our team managed to meet all the deadlines and to .... the .... that was allocated to the project.

Language review
Talking about the future

A These words and phrases refer to the future. Put them in order, starting with the soonest.

in four days' time ☐	next month ☐	the week after next ☐
in ten minutes [1]	next year ☐	tomorrow morning ☐
in three weeks' time ☐	the day after tomorrow ☐	tonight ☐

B Rewrite the sentences using the verbs in brackets.

1 We are going to visit the Trade Fair. (*plan*)
   ....*We are planning to visit the Trade Fair.*....

2 We are sure we will make a profit within three years. (*expect*)
   ....*We expect to make a profit within three years.*....

3 We are going to launch a new range next summer. (*intend*)
   ....

4 We will beat our competitors before long. (*hope*)
   ....

5 We are sure we will open three new subsidiaries before long. (*expect*)
   ....

6 We are going to open a new sales office in Bratislava. (*intend*)
   ....

C Look at Florian Straub's diary for next week and study the examples. Then complete the conversation between Jessica and Florian's secretary. It is now Friday 11th.

Mon 14		Thurs 17	
am	*visit Bielefeld factory*	am	*Geneva*
pm	*meet Korean visitors*	pm	
Tues 15		**Fri 18**	
am	*give talk on word-of-mouth advertising (9–10)*	am	*Geneva*
pm	*prepare departmental meeting*	pm	
Wed 16		**Sat 19**	
am	*departmental meeting (10.00–11.30)*	am	*Geneva*
pm	*to Geneva*	pm	*back from Geneva*

Examples:
• Florian Straub *is visiting* the Bielefeld factory on Monday morning.
• On Wednesday morning, he *is attending* a departmental meeting.

Jessica: Hello. I'd like to make an appointment to see Florian Straub on Wednesday afternoon.

Secretary: I'm afraid Mr Straub is .... [1] then. And he's not .... [2] until Saturday.

Jessica: Right. How about Monday?

Secretary: He's tied up all day Monday. Would Tuesday suit you?

Jessica: Tuesday? Fine. What sort of time?

Secretary: Well, he's .... [3] till 10.00, but he could see you after that. Otherwise in the afternoon he's .... [4] , but I'm sure he could fit you in.

Jessica: Three o'clock would be great.

Secretary: Three. Right. I've made a note of that, and I'll call you back to confirm the appointment.

Jessica: Thank you very much.

Writing
Linkers

A Look at the examples. Then answer the three questions below.

- Our new range of cosmetics is not doing very well. **For instance**, sales of our *Cleopatra* day cream have fallen by 20%.
- Our competitors are already working on new designs. **That is why** we should launch our new range as soon as possible.
- If they want to attract more tourists, they should increase the number of international flights. **In addition**, they should improve services.

Which linker (in **bold**) is used to:

- introduce an *explanation*? ....
- introduce an *example*? ....
- make an *additional point*? ....

B Complete each sentence with the best linker from exercise A.

1 There are different ways you could improve your performance. *For instance* , you could try to visit five customers a day instead of three.
2 I have informed everyone personally. .... , they have all read my report.
3 I have not met my sales targets. .... I am worried I will not get a bonus.
4 I want you to meet the deadlines we agreed on. .... , I expect you to hand in your report by Thursday.
5 Prices in the city centre have gone up. .... we should look for new office space in the suburbs.
6 Nizhny Novgorod is attracting more foreign investors. .... , a French company has recently invested $20m in a plant there.

Time management

C Kati Fekete is the manager of Lindcom Hungary. She is expecting three senior executives from Lindcom International Headquarters, Stockholm. Look at the schedule she has produced.

Wednesday May 24	
8.15	Arrival Ferihegy Airport
	Transfer to Majestic Hotel
11.00	Meet all staff, Budapest Office
	Buffet Lunch, Budapest Office
14.00	Sales Team: Performance Evaluation

Thursday May 25	
8.00	Meeting with Ms Ana Viktor, Sales Manager
10.00	Minibus to Lindcom Electronics in Hatvan
11.00	Tour of Lindcom Electronics/Meet staff
12.00	Lunch with local manager
13.30	Return to Budapest
	Free afternoon or guided city tour
18.30	Airport transfer
19.45	Departure for Stockholm

Kati receives this e-mail from Stockholm informing her about some changes. Complete the e-mail on page 35 with words from the box.

~~sending~~   are leaving   cannot   has to   have to   seeing

Language wor[

From: Per.Jonsson@lindcom.se
To: feketekati3@freemail.hu

Dear Kati,

Thanks for .... *sending* ....[1] the schedule.

Unfortunately, we ....[2] change our plans owing to unexpected problems here at headquarters.

We ....[3] leave on Wednesday 24 as we intended. Instead, we ....[4] for Budapest on Thursday 25 on the same flight, and returning to Stockholm on the Saturday morning.

The Performance Evaluation is very important – we want to have at least two full hours for that. The meeting with Ms Viktor ....[5] be after that, either later in the day or the day after; see which is more convenient.

Apart from that, feel free to make any other changes you like.

I apologise for the inconvenience this may cause you.

Looking forward to ....[6] you soon.

With best wishes,

Per

D **Write an e-mail (35 – 45 words) to all Sales staff.**

- Inform them of the change of time.
- Encourage everybody to be there.
- Apologise for possible inconvenience.

From: feketekati3@freemail.hu
To: All Sales staff   Date: 16th May
Subject: Visit from International Headquarters Stockholm

Unfortunately our guests from Stockholm...
....
....
....
....
....
....

Editing **E** **Read the text about setting up a business abroad.**

- In each line **1 – 8** there is **one wrong word**.
- For each line, **underline the wrong word** in the text and **write the correct word** in the space provided.

Deciding to move abroad to set up your own business is probably one of <u>a</u>	1 *the*
biggest decisions you will ever made. That is why you should plan your move	2 ....
well in advance. Firstly, it is a good idea to make several visit to the area where	3 ....
you intend to relocate. This will allow you to research your custom base, to	4 ....
assess local competition, and to make usefully business contacts.	5 ....
Secondly, you could begin to learn the language of the country were you want	6 ....
to go. As the way people doing business varies from one country to another, you	7 ....
also need to earn about the culture, about local customs and business etiquette.	8 ....

Managing people

Vocabulary

A Complete the first gap in the sentences below with a verb from Box A and the second gap with a preposition from Box B.

Box A
~~listen~~ communicate deal believe
invest respond delegate

Box B
~~to~~ in in to
to with with

Seven ways to manage people more successfully

1 Your staff will often have good ideas and suggestions, so ...*listen*... *to*.... what they have to say.

2 Do not think you have to do everything yourself. .... tasks .... other people.

3 Problems may be more difficult to solve if you wait too long, so .... them as soon as you can.

4 Good employees want to develop professionally, so .... courses and seminars for them.

5 Clear information is very important. .... your employees clearly, so that they know exactly what you expect.

6 When your employees are satisfied, they work more effectively, so .... their needs without delay.

7 And finally, remember that trust is essential. Your staff needs a manager that they can strongly ....

B Complete the sentences with the correct prepositions.

1 Staff often complained ...*about*... the new manager, saying he didn't believe ....*in*...... their abilities.

2 Robert was arguing .... his boss .... taxation.

3 Did she talk .... you .... her plans to leave the company?

4 Good. So you all seem to agree .... me .... the main points.

5 They apologised .... everyone .... their failure to deal .... the crisis.

6 The team had to report .... their progress .... the manager every month.

C Tick the correct sentences. Supply, correct or delete the prepositions where necessary.

1 Robert never listens my suggestions.
   Robert never listens to my suggestions.

2 Socialising colleagues is sometimes a good way to learn about what is happening in different departments.

3 Linda would like to discuss about the report's recommendations with you.

4 My company spends a lot of money for training courses for employees.

5 He may become a good manager. It depends of his communication skills.

6 The March conference accounted for 25% of our staff development budget.

Language review
Reported speech

A Put the words in the correct order to make a reported dialogue.

1 My/ready/wasn't/asked/my/why/me/boss/report
   My boss asked me why my report wasn't ready.

2 working/computer/I/my/properly/replied/wasn't

3 a/He/I/needed/new/one/said/that

4 also/ahead/Then/he/should/plan/to/said/try/I

5 organised/was/answered/well/I/usually/I/that

6 a/asked/computer/Finally,/get/him/I/I/new/when/would

B Check your answers to exercise A. Then complete the sentences with the actual words spoken.

1 'Why ..... *isn't your report ready* ... ?' asked my boss.

2 'Well, my computer .... ,' I replied.

3 'I think you .... ,' he said.

4 'And you should .... ,' he also said.

5 'But I'm .... ,' I answered.

6 'When .... ?' I asked finally.

C Correct the mistakes in two of sentences 2 – 6.

1 He told them invest in a good training course.
   He told them to invest in a good training course.

2 She said that gaining the staff's trust is important.

3 They asked him how he deal with those problems in his previous job.

4 She said I should communicate with colleagues more clearly.

5 She asked them to agree on a date for their next meeting.

6 He told that last month's sales figures were very good.

D Look at the examples. Then report the four questions below in the same way.

Wh- questions

• *What* do you want to do?
  He asked her *what* she wanted to do.

• *How much* do you earn?
  He asked her *how much* she earned.

Yes/No questions

• *Do* you plan ahead?
  He asked her *if* she planned ahead.

• *Could* you deal with a crisis?
  He asked her *if* she could deal with a crisis.

1 Do you adapt easily to new situations?
   He asked her ....

2 How often do you invest in courses?
   He asked her ....

3 Are you having difficulty contacting our consultant?
   He asked her ....

4 Why is this year's budget so small?
   He asked her ....

Language work

37

Language work

Writing
Preparing for report writing

A Match each sentence with a percentage from the box.

| 0% 4% 31% 48% 54% ~~73%~~ 94% 100% |

1 About three quarters of the staff — `73%`
2 Almost everybody/Most of the staff
3 Almost one third of the staff
4 Everybody
5 Hardly anybody
6 Just under half of the staff
7 More than half of the staff
8 Nobody

B Lindcom International's managers wanted to know if their employees think they are *good* managers. So they sent everyone a questionnaire.
Look at the summary of questionnaire findings and complete the conclusions section of the report with phrases from the box.

YOU AND YOUR MANAGER SUMMARY OF QUESTIONNAIRE FINDINGS			
	Often	Sometimes	Never
1 Does your manager listen to your suggestions?	5%	35%	60%
2 Does s/he respond to your concerns?	2%	73%	25%
3 Does s/he say 'well done'?	19%	34%	47%
4 Does s/he give you the information you need?	97%	2%	1%
5 Do you enjoy working with her/him?	33%	52%	15%

| ~~most of the staff~~ almost half one-third almost everybody a quarter of |

CONCLUSIONS

..Most of the staff..[1] are clearly dissatisfied with the way management listens to their suggestions. In addition, ...[2] the staff say their manager never responds to their concerns.

.....................[3] say that they often enjoy working with their manager. On the other hand, ...[4] say their manager never praises them.

On the positive side, ...[5] is satisfied with the way their manager communicates information.

Match the sentence halves to make the recommendations section of the report.

RECOMMENDATIONS

1 Management should build on its strengths
2 We must urgently look into ways of
3 Moreover, we should adopt
4 We should also remember to praise
5 As a result, our people would certainly enjoy

a) working with us more than they do at present.
b) and continue to communicate information efficiently.
c) our employees for their good work.
d) taking into account our employees' suggestions.
e) a more sympathetic attitude towards them.

Requesting information

D You work for Lindcom UK. Read the course advertisement below. Then choose the appropriate information (a – l) to complete the letter.

The Morningside Business & Administration Training College

MBATC

Forthcoming courses

Cultural Differences in the Workplace

The aim of this two-day workshop is to enable participants to understand cultural differences in order to improve relationships in the workplace.

Course fee: £150

Tutor: Fredrik Karlsson, MBA, PhD (Lund University)

Dates: to be advised

Venue: The Morningside BAT College
13 Buccleuch Avenue
Edinburgh EH4 7BG

For further details, write to Donald Strachan at the above address.

---

a) All the best,

b) Dear Mr Strachan

c) Hi Donald!

d) Dear Sir / Madam

e) Please write soon.

f) Sue Lowles,
Deputy Manager Lindcom UK

g) We look forward to hearing from you.

h) Yours faithfully

i) Lindcom UK
30 Burrard Street
Brentford TW9 2AK

j) 11 May

k) Mr Donald Strachan
The Morningside BAT College
13 Buccleuch Avenue
Edinburgh EH4 7BG

l) Yours sincerely

Language work

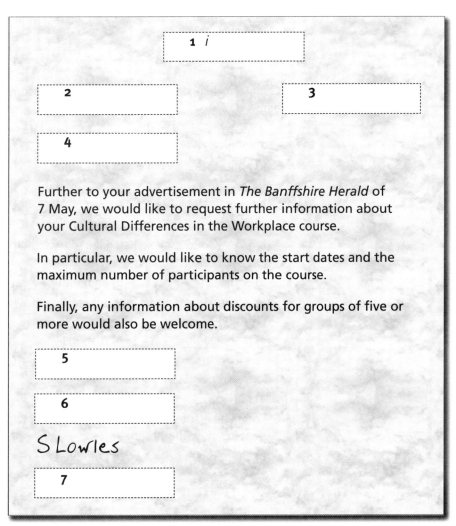

1 *i*

2

3

4

Further to your advertisement in *The Banffshire Herald* of 7 May, we would like to request further information about your Cultural Differences in the Workplace course.

In particular, we would like to know the start dates and the maximum number of participants on the course.

Finally, any information about discounts for groups of five or more would also be welcome.

5

6

S Lowles

7

Conflict

Vocabulary **A** Match the sentence halves.

Six tips for being a more successful negotiator

1 Good answers don't always come quickly,
2 Sometimes you have to compromise –
3 Don't get angry too quickly –
4 Don't agree with everyone all the time,
5 Say when you like an idea –
6 Keep the same attitude towards others –

a) you can't be tough all the time.
b) or they'll think you're weak.
c) enthusiastic negotiators are rare!
d) be consistent.
e) so don't be too impatient.
f) try to stay calm.

B Make the adjectives negative by adding the correct prefix from the box. Use a good dictionary to help you.

in- im- ir- un-

1 ..*un*.. sympathetic
2 .... patient
3 .... formal
4 .... responsible
5 .... cooperative

6 .... polite
7 .... responsive
8 .... emotional
9 .... critical
10 .... consistent

C Complete each sentence with the negative form of one of the three adjectives below it.

1 It was very ......*impolite*.......... to be late for the meeting and not even apologise.

a) polite   **b)** emotional   **c)** formal

2 He prefers .... meetings, where everybody can relax and feel comfortable.

a) patient   **b)** responsive   **c)** formal

3 It takes two to tango. They have to try to help and stop being so ....

a) critical   **b)** cooperative   **c)** credible

4 He signed the contract without reading it. What an .... attitude!

a) responsible   **b)** responsive   **c)** emotional

5 She'll criticise you one day and praise you the next. How can anyone be so .... ?

a) patient   **b)** consistent   **c)** emotional

6 I think he is too .... He seems to accept whatever people say, without thinking.

a) cooperative   **b)** credible   **c)** critical

Language review
Conditionals

A Match the question halves.

1 Wouldn't we seem impatient
2 Will you get a bonus
3 Won't you make a concession
4 Would you increase your order
5 Wouldn't they be disappointed
6 Will Ana ever win their trust

a) if she keeps being inconsistent?
b) if they didn't win the contract?
c) if you exceed the sales target?
d) if we told them to hurry again?
e) if we delivered immediately?
f) if they make one?

B Complete Speaker B's short answers.

1 A: Would you complain if they were late?
  B: Of course ....*I would*......... .

2 A: If we placed regular orders, would they cover transport costs?
  B: No, I'm afraid ....

3 A: Perhaps they'll be less impatient if we explain our situation.
  B: Yes, I'm sure ....

4 A: They wouldn't deliver faster even if we always paid cash.
  B: ....wouldn't. They've always been terribly slow.

5 A: If she comes this morning, will you talk to their representative?
  B: ....will.

6 A: Do you think he'd resign if he didn't win the contract?
  B: No, I'm sure ....

7 A: Will you inform us if there's a delay?
  B: Yes, ...

C Complete the sentences with *'ll, 'd, won't* or *wouldn't*.

1 I'm sure they ...*wouldn't*.. continue doing business with you if they weren't satisfied.
2 If he was able to deal with pressure, he .... be an excellent negotiator.
3 If I lose this order, I'm afraid it .... affect my commission.
4 If you don't increase the discount, we .... be able to increase the size of our order.
5 We .... have to turn to another supplier if you were able to deliver this month.
6 You .... get an extra day off even if you win this contract, I'm afraid.

D Complete the sentences with the correct form of the verbs in brackets.

1 We .*'ll give*......... (*give*) you a 15% discount if you pay cash.
2 If they .... (*pay*) late, we'd close their account.
3 If you .... (*deliver*) this week, we'll place a bigger order.
4 We .... (*deliver*) this week if you paid cash.
5 We'll give her a free gift if she .... (*increase*) her order.
6 If they make a concession, we .... (*do*) the same.
7 If you place regular orders, we .... (*cover*) insurance.
8 We would consider a bigger discount if you .... (*order*) a larger quantity.

Writing
Business letters

A People often start a business letter by saying why they are writing. Complete these typical opening sentences with the correct verb from the box.

> ~~confirm~~ complain enquire invite request

1 I am writing to ...*confirm*... the dates we agreed for our next meeting.
2 I would like to .... your advice.
3 I am writing to .... about the low quality of the goods you supplied.
4 I would like to .... you to visit our stand at the Trade Fair.
5 I would like to .... about the course advertised in the *Financial Times*.

B When you reply to a business letter, you usually begin by making reference to a previous communication.
Complete the beginning of the replies to the five letters in exercise A with a word from the box.

> ~~confirming~~ request enquiry complaint invitation

1 Thank you for .*confirming*. the dates ...
2 With reference to your .... for advice ...
3 With reference to your .... about the low quality ...
4 Thank you for your .... to visit your stand ...
5 With reference to your .... about the course ...

C Put the sentences in the fax in the correct order.

FAX   [page 1 of 1]

Mr S. Munroe
PHILLIP'S OFFICE SUPPLIES INTERNATIONAL
Level 8, 103 Berry Street
North Sydney NSW 2060

23 March

Dear Mr Munroe

SUN SING
ADVERTISING

1 PALMER STREET
WINDSOR
NSW 2756
TEL: (02) 4577 0285
FAX: (02) 4577 0286

OUR ORDER BG/503

a) As we urgently need those supplies, could you please send the correct items and pick up the wrong ones as soon as possible. ☐

b) However, you sent us toner cartridges for photocopiers instead of the laser jet ones we had ordered. ☐

c) We look forward to hearing from you. ☐

d) I am writing with reference to the above order for office supplies. ☑

e) In addition, three of the boxes contained different coloured paper. ☐

f) This morning we ordered 5 toner cartridges (Ref. LXJ2) and 10 boxes of white A4 photocopying paper (Ref. PA4/1). ☐

Yours sincerely

Mary Li

Mary Li

D Write a reply to the fax in exercise C. The Useful language box will help you.

FAX

[page 1 of 1]

PHILLIP'S OFFICE SUPPLIES INTERNATIONAL
Level 8, 103 Berry Street
North Sydney NSW 2060
Tel +61 2 9978 4040
Fax +61 2 9978 5050

Sun Sing Advertising
1 Palmer Street
Windsor NSW 2756

26 March

Dear Ms Li

....
....
....

Yours sincerely

Steve Munroe

Steve Munroe
Head of Customer Service

Useful language

Opening
- Further to your ...
- With reference to your ...
- Thank you for your ....

Apologising
- We would like to apologise for the problems you had.
- Once again, our apologies for the inconvenience you had.

Explaining
- I am afraid there was a mix-up over your order.

Promising action
- The goods will be sent by special delivery.

Closing
- We look forward to receiving further orders from you.
- We very much hope that you will continue to do business with us.

Editing **E** Read the text about the influence of culture on negotiating behaviour.
- In each line **1 – 8** there is **one wrong word**.
- For each line, **underline the wrong word** in the text and **write the correct word** in the space provided.

Many people say that negotiating behaviour varies from one culture to another.	
Americans, they say, are usually open, sociable and informal. <u>Germans</u>	1 *German*
negotiators, on the other hand, placing great weight on clarity and thoroughness,	2 ....
while Spaniards are spontaneous and did not mind interrupting each other.	3 ....
There is probably any truth in such generalisations, but we should be very	4 ....
careful with culturally stereotypes. To begin with, they may affect the way we	5 ....
respond on other nationalities. More importantly, we should remember that	6 ....
each negotiator have a unique personality. We notice this more quickly when	7 ....
doing business with people from the same country like ours.	8 ....

New business

Vocabulary

A **Complete each sentence with an appropriate economic term from the box.**

> ~~interest rate~~   balance of trade   exchange rate
> gross domestic product (GDP)   government bureaucracy   inflation rate
> tax incentives   labour force   foreign investment   unemployment rate

1 If you plan to borrow money, you will want to know the ...*interest rate*... .

2 In countries where the .... is high, young people tend to study more.

3 How many yen to the euro? Do you know the .... , by any chance?

4 According to a recent survey, 12% of the .... are earning less than the minimum wage.

5 So many forms to fill in just to import one photocopier! Nobody needs all this ....

6 The higher the .... of a country, the richer its people are.

7 When the value of a country's exports is greater than the value of its imports, we say that the .... is 'favourable'.

8 Prices increased again last month, so the .... rose to 5.3%.

9 Less government bureaucracy will encourage ....

10 The government is offering attractive .... to encourage foreign investment.

B **Match the economic terms (1 – 6) to their definitions (a – f).**

1 foreign debt

2 public expenditure

3 recession

4 subsidies

5 trade deficit

6 trade surplus

a) the total amount of money spent by a government on schools, roads, the army, etc.

b) money that a country owes to lenders abroad

c) situation when a country sells more goods to other countries than it buys from other countries

d) situation when a country pays more money for imports than it gets from exports

e) money that a government pays to make something cheaper to buy

f) a period when trade and business activity decreases

C **Complete the sentences with an economic term from exercise B.**

1 To help farmers, the EU has given out millions of euros in agricultural ....

2 The country was able to repay some of its loans from abroad and so reduce its ....

3 Industrial production is still decreasing. It seems that the country is heading for a ....

Language review
Time clauses

A **Correct the four sentences which are wrong. The first one has been done for you.**

1 We can't invest in that country until their economy will be stable.
   We can't invest in that country until their economy is stable.

2 I'll let you know as soon as I receive their new brochure.

3 I'll let you know as soon as I've received their new brochure.

4 We'll phone you when the goods will be here.

5 When we've discussed the contract, we can close the meeting.

6 When we discuss the contract, we must ask about transport costs.

7 We'll deal with insurance after they will tell us about their special discount.

8 Our guests would like to visit the unit before they will go back to Qatar.

9 Before they sign this contract, they want us to promise better terms for future business.

10 I don't recommend investing there until they've reduced government bureaucracy.

B **Match the two parts of each dialogue.**

1 A: When do you want to discuss the project?

2 A: Have you read Peter's sales report?

3 A: So have they won the contract, then?

4 A: It seems we're not doing business with Alfatex anymore.

5 A: It would be useful to know today's exchange rates.

6 A: These figures need checking.

7 A: Are you going to the Trade Fair now?

a) B: No, never again. Certainly not until they apologise for their terrible mistakes.

b) B: We don't know yet. We'll have information after we've talked to the team leader.

c) B: Yes, I agree. We'll find out as soon as we get the *FT*.

d) B: Yes, I have. I'd like to discuss it with you when you have a minute.

e) B: Yes, I am. If anybody phones while I'm out, tell them I'll be back by 1.30.

f) B: Well, could we possibly do that before the meeting starts?

g) B: When you've typed them all up, we can check them together.

C **Make one sentence from the two sentences given.**

1 We'll meet all the candidates. Then we'll decide how many to employ.
   After we've .....*met all the candidates, we'll decide how many to employ*..... .

2 Julia will finish her report soon. I want to see it immediately.
   I .... as soon as ....

3 I will not invite them anymore. They must apologise first.
   I .... until ....

4 Perhaps we'll employ him. Let's contact his referees first.
   Let's .... before ....

5 I'll type up the report. Then I'll give you a copy.
   I'll .... when I've ....

6 You'll be on the plane. Read the contracts then.
   .... when ....

7 Prices are going to increase soon. Let's buy now.
   .... before ....

8 We'll win the contract. We'll inform our shareholders immediately.
   As soon as ...., ...

Writing
Linkers

A Match each government measure with its purpose.

Government measures	Purpose
1 create free training programmes	a) attract foreign investors
2 make exports easier	b) stimulate consumer spending
3 pass a very strict environmental law	c) reduce the budget deficit
4 raise taxes	d) reduce unemployment
5 lower the interest rate	e) improve the balance of trade
6 try to reduce bureaucracy	f) stop companies polluting air and water

B Express the ideas in exercise A in one sentence, using the linker *in order to*.

1 In order to reduce unemployment, the government is creating free training programmes.
or The government is creating free training programmes in order to reduce unemployment.

2 The government is making ....
....

3 In order to stop companies ....
....

4 ....
....

5 ....
....

6 ....
....

Report writing

C Study the table. Then correct the four numerical mistakes in the report about men employed. The first one has been done for you.

People employed in three industries by gender				
	Percentages			
	Men		Women	
	1989	1999	1989	1999
Manufacturing	33	25	20	10
Health, education and public administration services	16	20	40	45
Financial and business services	10	15	10	20

Report   *quarter*
- A third of all men employed were in manufacturing in 1989, compared with only a ~~fifth~~ in 1999.
- On the other hand, around one in eight men employed were in health, education and public administration services in 1989, while the same industry accounted for one-fifth of men's jobs in 1999.
- As regards the percentage of men employed in financial and business services, it increased from 12 in 1989 to 15 twenty years later.

D Use the report in exercise C to write a similar report about *women* employed.

Report

• One-fifth of all women employed ....
....
....
....
....

• On the other hand, ...
....
....
....
....

• As regards the percentage ....
....
....
....
....

Editing

E Read this economic profile about a country.

• In most of the lines **1 – 13** there is **one extra word** which does not fit. Some lines, however, are correct.
• If a line is **correct**, put a tick (✓) in the space provided.
• If there is an **extra word** in the line, write that word in the space.

Our country has become a completely modern market	1	....✓........
economy. It is characterised by high-tech agriculture, the	2	....*the*......
up-to-date industry, and an extensive government welfare	3	....
measures. Other features include very good living and	4	....
standards, as well as high dependence on their foreign trade.	5	....
We export food and the energy and have a comfortable	6	....
balance of payments surplus. The government has reduced	7	....
so the formerly high unemployment rate and maintained low	8	....
inflation and a stable currency. It has also lowered income	9	....
tax rates and raised environmental taxes. This way so, it has	10	....
been able to maintain overall but tax revenues. Finally, in	11	....
order to deal with long-term demographic changes which	12	....
could reduce the labour force, the government it has	13	....
introduced a number of labour market reforms.		

12 Products

Vocabulary

A **Read the sentences and supply the missing vowels for each adjective.**

1 A product that is *p _ p _ l _ r* is enjoyed or liked by a lot of people.

2 A product that is *r _ l _ _ bl _* can be trusted to work well.

3 If a product is *_ c _ n _ m _ c _ l*, it doesn't cost a lot of money to use.

4 An *_ ttr _ ct _ v _* product is one that people find beautiful and exciting.

5 A product that is *f _ sh _ _ n _ bl _* is popular at a particular time.

6 You say that a product is *_ n _ q _ _* if it is very unusual or special.

B **Complete each sentence with a word from the box.**

~~quality~~ lasting made selling tech wearing

1 Rolex makes high-.....*quality*.... watches.

2 Timberland makes fashionable and hard-................ boots.

3 Dell manufactures high-................ computer products.

4 Nokia has produced some best-................ mobile phones.

5 Tungsram makes long-................ light bulbs.

6 Samsonite sells practical and well-................ bags and suitcases.

C **Make new adjectives by joining a word from Box A to a word from Box B. Then complete the definitions.**

Box A
~~up~~ down custom first multi

Box B
~~market~~ purpose class market made

1 An *upmarket*.. product is expensive and usually of high quality.

2 If products are .... - .... , they are made specially for one person or group of people.

3 A .... - .... product is one that has several different uses.

4 .... products are cheap and sometimes not good quality.

5 .... - .... products are of excellent quality.

D **Complete the text with the best words from page 49.**

The life cycle of a product

All products have a life cycle. Therefore, new products are being developed all the time to replace older products which are coming to the end of their lives.

The cycle begins when a new product is *b.*[1]. At that stage, there is only a plan or a drawing, which is then used when the product is .....[2]. Nobody knows how well the new product works, or how good it is, so it has to be .....[3]. On the basis of the test results, it may have to be modified.

Once the necessary .....[4] have been made, the product is ready to be launched and then .....[5] in a number of advertising campaigns. Advertising plays a very important role, and so does .....[6]. Indeed, the company has to make sure that its new product is .....[7] to as many customers as possible. Finally, when it is clear that sales are going down steadily, the company will probably decide to .....[8] the product.

---

1 **a)** planned	**b)** designed	**c)** sketched
2 **a)** fabricated	**b)** manufactured	**c)** assembled
3 **a)** tested	**b)** examined	**c)** researched
4 **a)** specifications	**b)** qualities	**c)** improvements
5 **a)** promoted	**b)** exhibited	**c)** displayed
6 **a)** discount	**b)** delivering	**c)** distribution
7 **a)** profitable	**b)** available	**c)** marketable
8 **a)** destroy	**b)** discontinue	**c)** distinguish

Language review
Passives

A Match the sentence halves. Then underline the passive forms.

1 If sales continue to fall

2 Most of the world's soccer balls are made in Asia

3 Our new computer games will be distributed

4 The existing model can be improved easily,

5 The packaging will be modified

6 When Alkaphen was launched,

a) and our product will become a lot more environment friendly.

b) the competition was already testing a similar drug.

c) I'm afraid this model will have to be discontinued.

d) nationwide well before the advertising campaign begins.

e) so we don't have to design a new product.

f) by very young people who live in poverty.

B Make these sentences passive. Use *by* only if it is important to say who did the action.

1 They make Suzuki cars in Hungary too.
Suzuki cars are made in Hungary too.

2 Someone is repairing your washing machine now.

3 Bayer developed this new drug.

4 They were still researching into the effects of Alkaphen.

5 Bayer has retained all selling rights.

6 The question is, have we promoted our new range enough?

7 If sales continue to fall, we will have to discontinue it.

8 We should test this new product immediately.

9 We could improve its distribution.

10 We definitely have to improve the packaging.

C Use a passive form of the verbs in the box to link the sentence beginnings (1 – 6) with the endings (a – f), as in the example.

~~make~~ do test consume create invent

1 Casucci jeans

2 In the future, a lot more shopping

3 Nestlé food products

4 The 'little black dress'

5 The telephone

6 They claim that none of their new cosmetics

a) by A. G. Bell.

b) by millions of people every day.

c) by Chanel, the French fashion designer.

d) of high-quality denim.

e) on animals.

f) online.

Example:
1 – d: *Casucci jeans are made of high-quality denim.*

Language work

Writing
Linkers

A Study the example sentences, and notice the words used to link them. Then link sentences 1 – 4 in a similar way.

- A fashion designer created the 'little black dress'. *She* was a genius.

  The fashion designer *who* created the 'little black dress' was a genius.

- A brand is a name. *It* makes it easy for customers to recognise a product.

  A brand is a name *that/which* makes it easy for customers to recognise a product.

- A warehouse is a large building. Goods are stored *there* until they are distributed to shops to be sold.

  A warehouse is a large building *where* goods are stored until they are distributed to shops to be sold.

- A recession is a period of time. The economy is doing badly *then*.

  A recession is a period of time *when* the economy is doing badly.

1 This new instant coffee has been produced by a well-known company. The company has always sold its coffee in the higher price ranges.

   ....

   ....

2 The shop floor is an area in a factory. Ordinary workers do their work there.

   ....

3 A retailer is a person. She or he owns or runs a shop selling goods to members of the public. ....

   ....

4 Sick leave is a period of time. You stay away from your job because you are ill then. ....

   ....

Enquiring about a product

B Complete the advertisement for a new product with phrases from the box.

~~user-friendly~~	including	market leader
run	further information	high-performance

Just Scan It!

At ScanIt International we spend a lot of effort making our products as ......user-friendly....... ¹ **as possible.**

*Our new scanner Alpha JTX2 continues that trend .
Alpha JTX2 will help you* .... ² *your business
smoothly and efficiently. It is a* .... ³
scanner designed for those who need documents in a hurry

- *Get professional results in seconds*
- *High-resolution scanning*
- *Automatic document feeder (up to 30 sheets)*
- *Copies up to ten pages per minute*
- *One-touch buttons for e-mailing images to colleagues or publishing them on a website.*

Alpha JTX2:
the .... ⁴
in scanning technology.

Only £199,
.... ⁵
*adaptor for slides
and negatives.*

For .... ⁶ **and a free trial, call
freefone 0800 427 8732 or e-mail us at <scanit@hitech.co.uk>**

C Write an e-mail to ScanIt International on behalf of your company to request further information about the scanner described in exercise B.

Organise your message like this:

1 Start with Dear Sir/Madam.

2 Say where you saw the advertisement.

3 Ask what you need to know:

   a) Can the JTX2 scan 3-D objects?

   b) What types of paper can be used?

4 Say you are interested in a free trial and ask how long the trial period is.

5 Finish your message with a suitable ending.

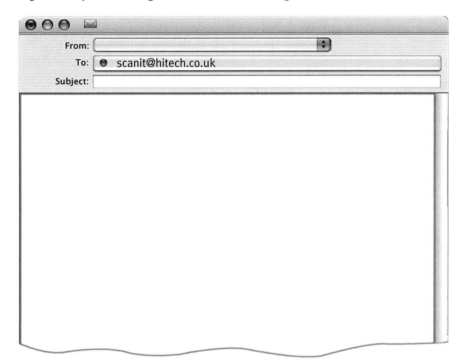

```
From: [                                    ] ▼
To: ● scanit@hitech.co.uk
Subject: [                                    ]
```

Language work

Editing **D** Read the text about launching a new product.

• In each line **1 – 6** there is **one wrong word**.

• For each line, **underline the wrong word** in the text and **write the correct word** in the space provided.

Are you planning to launch a new product or service? If you are, remember that

not only *what* you say about it is <u>importance</u>, but also *how* you say it. You   **1** *important*

should try to emphasise the features of your product which not other product   **2** ....

have, i.e., its *unique selling point*. You should also try to describe the   **3** ....

benefits of your goods or services from your costumiers' perspective.   **4** ....

Successful business people usually know or at least have a good idea of what they   **5** ....

customers want or need. These knowledge can be very useful in building   **6** ....

customer satisfaction and loyalty.

Talk business

The aim of this *Talk business* section is to make you more aware of some of the main features of English pronunciation. This will help you understand spoken English more easily. It can also help you discover areas you may need to work on for your spoken English to sound more natural.

The sounds of English

🎧 **Look, listen and repeat.**

Vowel sounds

/ɪ/	quick fix	/ɔː/	short course
/iː/	clean sheet	/ʊ/	good books
/e/	sell well	/uː/	school rules
/æ/	bad bank	/ʌ/	much luck
/ɑː/	smart card	/ɜː/	first term
/ɒ/	top job	/ə/	a'bout 'Canada

Diphthongs

/eɪ/	play safe	/əʊ/	go slow
/aɪ/	my price	/ɪə/	near here
/ɔɪ/	choice oil	/eə/	fair share
/aʊ/	downtown	/ʊə/	tour

Consonants

1 Contrasting voiceless and voiced consonants

Voiceless		Voiced	
/p/	pay	/b/	buy
/f/	file	/v/	value
/t/	tax	/d/	deal
/θ/	think	/ð/	this
/tʃ/	cheap	/dʒ/	job
/s/	sell	/z/	zero
/k/	card	/g/	gain
/ʃ/	option	/ʒ/	decision

2 Other consonants

/m/	mine	/l/	loss	/n/	net	/r/	rise
/ŋ/	branding	/w/	win	/h/	high	/j/	year

Tips

- Identify the sounds that you have difficulty recognising or producing and focus mainly on these.
- Add your own key words in the Sounds of English section for the sounds you wish to focus on.
- Using the pause button on your cassette or CD player will give you time to speak or write when you do the exercises.

Using a dictionary

Any good dictionary today gives you useful information on the pronunciation of individual words. With the help of the *Longman Business English Dictionary* or the *Longman Wordwise Dictionary*, for example, you will be able to work out the pronunciation of any English word on your own, once you are familiar with the phonemic symbols.

In addition, a dictionary also gives you essential information about *word stress*. When a word has more than one syllable, we always put more stress on one of the syllables, that is, we say that syllable more strongly. Look at the dictionary entry for *compete*:

> **com•pete** /kəm'piːt/ *v* [I] to try to win something or to be more successful than someone else:

The sign ' shows you that the syllable immediately after it should be stressed: comPETE.
You will find various exercises on word stress in units 7, 8 and 9.

The sign ː shows you that the vowel is long. The contrast between *long* and *short* vowels is very important for mutual understanding.
In unit 1, for example, you will find an exercise on /ɪ/ and /iː/, while unit 11 has an exercise on /ɒ/ and /ɔː/.

Sounds and spelling

In English, (a) the same sound can be spelt in different ways, or (b) the same letters can be pronounced in different ways.

(a) Consider for example /əʊ/, the sound of *go slow*. It can be spelt *o* as in **open**, *oa* as in **loan**, *oe* as in **toe**, *ough* as in **although**, *ow* as in **know**, or *eou* as in **Seoul**.

(b) Take the letter *u*, for instance. It can be pronounced /ʌ/ as in **cut**, /ʊ/ as in **full**, /ɜː/ as in **turn**, /ɔː/ as in **sure**, /uː/ as in **tune**, or /ɪ/ as in **busy**.

Put the words from the box under the correct sound in the table below (the letters in bold show the sound).

break	**Eu**rope	in**s**urance	ad**v**ice	tr**ai**n
b**uy**er	frien**d**ship	know**l**edge	s**ai**d	w**a**nt
chair	h**ea**rt	l**augh**	**sc**ientific	th**ei**r
con**sc**ious		mi**lli**on		h**eigh**t

Vowels

/ɒ/	/e/	/ɑː/
1 job	1 sell	1 card
2	2	2 ....
3	3	3 ....

/eɪ/	/eə/	/aɪ/
1 pay	1 share	1 price
2	2	2 ....
3	3	3 ....

Consonants

/ʃ/	/s/	/j/
1 option	1 sell	1 year
2	2	2 ....
3	3	3 ....

A variety of sound–spelling relationships are explored in units 2, 6, 7, 8 and 9.

Shadowing

Shadowing is a very effective way to make the most of the recorded material.

1 Play a short section – a few words or one line of a dialogue – and then pause.

2 Without speaking, repeat internally what you heard.

3 Play the same section again. Pause and speak the words in exactly the same way and at the same speed. Repeat this step until you are completely satisfied with your performance.

4 Play the same section again and speak along with the voice on the recording. This is shadowing.

5 Move on to the next short section of the recording and repeat the same procedure.

Introduction

53

UNIT 1   Careers

Individual sounds

A **1.1 Listen to the difference between /ɪ/ and /iː/.**

/ɪ/	/iː/
Tim	team
pick	peak
bit	beat

B **Put the words from the box into the correct column, according to the pronunciation of the letter(s) in bold.**

| manager   teacher   mechanic   editor   policeman   art dealer |

/ɪ/as in quick fix	/iː/ as in clean sheet
. . . .	. . . .
. . . .	. . . .
. . . .	. . . .

1.2 Check your answers. Then listen and practise saying the words.

Connected speech

1.3 Listen to the pronunciation of *can / can't*.

She can speak Arabic. She can't speak Greek.
She can speak Arabic, but she can't speak Greek.

What's the rule?

• Within a sentence, a weak form of *can* is often used: /kən/ or /kn/.
• *Can't* is usually pronounced /kɑːnt/ in British English.

Practise saying the sentences.

1 He can use Visual Basic, but he can't use Java.
2 She can't start this week, but she can start by the end of the month.
3 I can't speak Mandarin fluently, but I can understand a lot.
4 We can let you know next week, but we can't promise anything.
5 She can use spreadsheets, but she can't design a website.

1.4 Now listen to the recording and 'shadow' (see page 53) the five sentences.

Stress and intonation

C **1.5 Listen to how these questions are spoken.**

1 Can you hold?
2 Did you say R-E-I-T-H?
3 Hello. Is that John Reith?
4 Could you take a message?
5 Could you tell me your name and address?

Tip

A *yes /no* question is usually asked with the voice going **up** at the end.

1.5 Listen again and practise saying the questions.

Telephoning

A 🎧 1.6 **Listen and complete the phrases.**

1 Can I ...*have*........ your name?
2 Just one .... , please.
3 Hold ....
4 I'd .... to speak to Ms Allan.
5 I'm .... she's in a meeting just now.
6 Can I .... a message?
7 Could you ask her to call me .... this afternoon?

🎧 1.6 **Listen again and practise saying the phrases.**

B 🎧 1.7 **Listen and complete each column with the missing letters of the alphabet.**

/eɪ/ as in play safe	/iː/ as in clean sheet	/e/ as in sell well	/aɪ/ as in my price	/əʊ/ as in go slow	/uː/ as in school rules	/ɑː/ as in smart card
...*a*...	..*b*... .*g*...	..*f*....	......	......	......	......
...*h*..	..*c*...	..*l*....	......	......	......	
......	..*d*...	....			......	
......	..*e*...	......				

> **Tips**
>
> Key words help you remember the pronunciation of each letter of the alphabet.
>
> When dictating or taking down a strange word, you need to know how to pronounce each letter of the alphabet clearly and accurately.

C 🎧 1.8 **Listen to the excerpts from phone conversations and write down the words that are spelt out.**

1 Name: 4 Company name:
2 Address: 5 Name:
3 Street name:

🎧 1.9 **Listen to these examples.**

	International code	Country code	Area code	Subscriber's number
1	00	Slovenia: 386	Ljubljana: 61	24661 87
2	00	Turkey: 90	Istanbul: 212	613 3367

D 🎧 1.10 **Listen to the excerpts and write down the phone numbers.**

1 If you'd like more details, please call our Bucharest office on ....
2 And our number in Tunis is ....
3 Please contact our Montevideo subsidiary. The country code is 598, and their number is ....
4 Yes, we do have an office in Madrid. The number is .... The country code is 34, by the way, and then 91 for Madrid.
5 Our agent in Bratislava can be reached on ....

> **Tips**
>
> Phone numbers are pronounced in groups. The digits are said separately.
>
> At the end of each group your voice goes up, except for the last group, when your voice goes down to signal that it is the end of the number.

Survival business English

UNIT 2 — Selling online

Individual sounds

A 🎧 **2.1 Listen carefully to how the letters in bold are pronounced in the following words. Indicate whether they sound the same (✓) or different (✗).**

1 ret**ai**ler p**ay**ment exch**a**nged ✓
2 ref**u**nd disc**ou**nt **o**ffer ✗
3 meth**o**d **o**ffer st**o**ck
4 ret**ur**n s**er**vice p**ur**chase
5 gr**o**ceries cl**o**thes neg**o**tiate
6 desp**a**tch s**a**les exch**a**nge

B **Look at the pronunciation chart (page 52) and complete these sentences with the correct symbol.**

1 *Discount* has the sound / .... / as in *downtown*.
2 *Method* has the sound / .... / as in *a'bout 'Canada*.
3 *Despatch* has the sound / .... / as in *bad bank*.

Connected speech

C 🎧 **2.2 Listen and complete the sentences.**

1 Online retailers have to .... secure guarantees to the public.
2 We have to .... some photocopying paper.
3 Their site is easy to visit. You don't have to ....
4 You'll have to .... on receipt of the goods.
5 They'll have to .... their website.

🎧 **2.2 Listen and check your answers. Notice how *have to* is pronounced.**

What's the rule?

- *Have to* is usually spoken as one word.
- Before a vowel sound (sentences 1 and 2), it is often pronounced / 'hæftʊ/.
- Before a consonant sound (3, 4 and 5), it is often pronounced / 'hæftə/.

🎧 **2.2 Listen again and practise saying the sentences.**

Stress and intonation

D 🎧 **2.3 Listen to the sentences.**

↗	↘
1 If we want them to finish this month,	they'll have to work weekends.
2 If they have to work weekends,	they'll need to be paid overtime.
3 If they're paid overtime,	our production costs will increase.
4 If our production costs increase,	we may have to raise our prices.
5 If we raise our prices again,	no one knows what will happen.

Tip

Notice the rising intonation at the end of the first part, and the falling intonation at the end of the second part.

🎧 **2.3 Listen again and practise saying the sentences.**

Sound work

Negotiating

A **Put the lines a) – g) of the negotiation into a suitable sequence.**

a) Right. Let's get started, shall we? If we buy 100 'Hit' and 200 'Tournament' tennis rackets, what discount can you offer us? `[1]`

b) All right, we'll agree to that. Now, if we place an order this week, will you be able to deliver the goods within two weeks? ☐

c) Fine. That's it, then. I think we've covered everything. ☐

d) Mmm, let me think about that. If we agree to let you pay by letter of credit, then you'll have to pay within 30 days, and you'll have to cover insurance as well. ☐

e) On an order of that size, and since it's your first order with us, we can offer 5%. But then we can offer 10% off all quoted prices for further orders above €6,000. `[2]`

f) Well, we'd prefer to pay by letter of credit. ☐

g) Certainly. And as regards payment, we would expect you to pay by bank transfer as soon as the goods have been despatched. ☐

B 🎧 **2.4 Listen and check your answers. Then listen again and spot four differences between the recording and the text in exercise A.**

C **Match each item 1 – 5 with an appropriate response a) – e).**

1 If we order 200 units, will you give us a 10% discount?

2 We would expect you to cover insurance as well.

3 We'd like you to deliver immediately.

4 We'll ship the goods by train. Is that all right?

5 You'll have to pay us in advance this time.

a) We'd rather you shipped them by road, in fact.

b) I'm sorry, but that's not acceptable. We can just guarantee delivery within ten days.

c) Sorry, but we can't agree to that. We can only cover freight.

d) Well, we'd prefer to pay you on delivery as usual.

e) I'm afraid we can only offer 5% on orders of that size.

D 🎧 **2.5 Listen and check your answers. Then listen again, and focus on the way speakers a) – e) respond.**

Tips

When we give a negative answer, we do not usually say just 'No'.

Instead, we often use phrases like these:

We'd rather …

I'm sorry, but …

Well, we'd prefer …

I'm afraid …

We also generally *explain* why we respond negatively.

🎧 **2.5 Listen again and practise saying the responses.**

Survival business English

UNIT 3   Companies

A 🎧 **3.1 Listen to how the verbs are pronounced.**

1 syllable	deals	makes
2 syllables	involves	recruits
3 syllables	finances	develops

B 🎧 **3.2 Listen to the recording. How many syllables do you hear?**

1   raises   ..2..
2   starts   .....
3   employs   .....
4   delivers   .....
5   improves   .....
6   increases   .....
7   costs   .....
8   produces   .....

🎧 **3.2 Listen again and practise saying the words.**

C   **List all the verbs in exercises A and B which end in /ɪz/.**

1   ... *finances* ....
2   ....
3   ....
4   ....

🎧 **3.3 Listen and check your answers.**

Connected speech

D 🎧 **3.4 Listen to the way *are* is pronounced in these sentences.**

1   We need people who are reliable.
2   The chocolates are made in Turin.
3   Our new products are not selling well.

Tip

We often use the weak form /ə/ when *are* appears within the sentence.

🎧 **3.4 Listen again and practise saying the sentences.**

E 🎧 **3.5 Listen and complete the sentences.**

1   .... good progress.
2   .... luxury chocolates.
3   .... a lot of business with India.
4   .... quite well this year.
5   .... ten new products every year.
6   .... a new computer system.

🎧 **3.5 Check your answers. Then listen again and practise saying the sentences.**

Sound work

A Complete the company description with words from the box.

achieved	rose	leading	located	operate

Zengő Furniture Company Rt. (ZFC Rt.) specialises in manufacturing and retailing office furniture. Based in Pécsvárad, in the south of Hungary, we are the . . . . [1] Hungarian company in our field. We . . . . [2] eight stores . . . . [3] throughout the country and employ 145 people altogether.

Last year our sales . . . . [4] to over 40 million euros, which represents a 19% increase over the previous year. Our earnings before interest and tax were 4.9 million euros, or 12% of sales. This result is better than the result we . . . . [5] the year before, when the margin was equal to 8.7% of sales.

🎧 **3.6 Listen and check your answers.**

B 🎧 **3.7 Listen and complete the fact sheet below.**

You will hear an interview with Pierre Chevrel, the General Manager of Espace Mode. Use up to three words or a number in each space.

ᔕᘿ Espace Mode ᘿᔕ
COMPANY FACT SHEET

Location:	. . . . . Grenoble . . . . . [1]
Main activity:	Clothes manufacturers and . . . . [2]
Customers:	Men and women from all walks of life in the . . . . [3] 16 – 25. We also . . . . [4] to agents and mail order catalogues.
Market position:	We are among the French . . . . [5] in the clothing sector.
Staff:	We employ nearly . . . . [6] people.
Financial information:	Annual turnover of over . . . . [7] million euros.
	Profits of . . . . [8] million euros, i.e., ... [9] of sales.
Future plans:	We're working on exciting new designs which will reflect a completely new concept . . . . [10]. *Espace Mode* is set to become . . . . [11] of the European fashion market.

C Use the fact sheet in exercise B to prepare a business presentation about Espace Mode. Use the tip and the Useful language box to help you.

Useful language

Introducing	Turning to a new topic	Concluding
I'd like to start by saying ...	Now I'd like to turn to ...	Finally, a few words about ...
I'm going to talk about ...	If we can now look at ...	So, to sum up ...
My main objectives are ...	What I'd like to talk about now is ...	In conclusion ...
The aim of my presentation is to ...	The next point I'd like to raise is ...	I would like to conclude by ...
The purpose of this presentation is to ...	What we've got to pay attention to now is ...	Now let me summarise the main points again.

UNIT 4 — Great ideas

A Look at the verbs and tick the pairs where the *-ed* endings sound the same.

1	started	decided	☑
2	developed	introduced	☐
3	exploited	discussed	☐
4	received	launched	☐
5	used	changed	☐
6	finished	stopped	☐

B 🎧 4.1 **Listen and check your answers. Then listen again and practise saying the verbs.**

C 🎧 4.2 **Listen to how the verb forms are pronounced.**

1 syllable	moved	asked	touched
2 syllables	prepared	reduced	wanted
3 syllables	attracted	discovered	established

D How many syllables do the verb forms have?

1	preferred	...*2*....	5	offered	....
2	helped	....	6	earned	....
3	financed	....	7	worked	....
4	adapted	....	8	advertised	....

🎧 4.3 **Check your answers. Then listen to the recording and practise saying the words.**

Connected speech

E 🎧 4.4 **Listen and complete the conversations.**

1 A: ......*Were*.......... they ....*trying*....... to develop a new drug?

   B: Well, everybody thinks they were.

2 A: She .... around the world on her own.

   B: Are you sure she was?

3 A: Our competitors .... their range of products very well.

   B: Weren't they really?

4 A: The new product .... a lot of customers.

   B: Well, in fact I think it was.

5 A: He .... the next advertising campaign.

   B: Yeah, and he was designing a new product at the same time.

Tips

Pronunciation of *was* and *were*

- In positive sentences *was* and *were* are usually pronounced /wəz/ and /wə/.
- At the beginning or at the end of a sentence, *was* and *were* are usually pronounced /wɒz/ and /wɜː/.
- *Wasn't* and *weren't* are always pronounced /'wɒznt/ and /wɜːnt/.

🎧 4.4 **Listen again and practise saying the sentences.**

Meetings

A 🎧 **4.5 Listen to eight extracts from meetings and decide what each speaker is doing.**
Write one letter, a) – d), next to the number of the speaker. Use each letter twice.

Speaker 1: ......*b*........
Speaker 2: ....
Speaker 3: ....
Speaker 4: ....
Speaker 5: ....
Speaker 6: ....
Speaker 7: ....
Speaker 8: ....

a) stating the aim
b) changing the topic
c) asking for comments
d) summarising

B 🎧 **4.6 Listen to the recording and complete the extracts from meetings.**

1 Right. Let's now ...*have a look*...... at our sales figures.
2 I'm not very happy about that, ...
3 Just a minute, ...
4 .... get started?
5 Let's get .... business.
6 Well, I'm not .... that.
7 What exactly .... by 'specialist stores'?
8 I'm .... launching the product just before summer.

C **These are the opening lines of a meeting. Put them in the right order 1 – 7.**

a) As you know, we're going to launch a very special new product – a unique soft drink with low sugar and carbon dioxide content. [2]

b) Firstly, we still have to decide when exactly we should launch the product. ☐

c) I've called this meeting for two main reasons. ☐

d) Sania, what do you think would be the best date? ☐

e) Secondly, we need your ideas for a new name, as many of you are not very happy with the name *Vitafruit*. ☐

f) Shall we begin? [1]

g) So, let's turn to the launch date. ☐

🎧 **4.7 Listen and check your answers. Then listen again and find three differences between the recording and the script.**

UNIT 5 Stress

A 🎧 **5.1 Listen and add the missing letters to the words.**

1 p̲r̲essure; _ _o_ _em; _ _omotion
2 wor_ _oad; li_ _ _ _yle; dea_ _ine
3 co_ _ _a_ _ _; a_ _ _; psychologi_ _ _
4 He resi_ _ _ _ three mo_ _ _ _ ago.
5 It's a _ _udy about _ _ _ess in the wor_ _ _ace.
6 She's pla_ _ _ _ lo_ _ of proje_ _ _.

> **Tip**
>
> Many English words have groups of two, three or four consonant sounds pronounced together. Pronouncing those groups of consonants correctly often requires a lot of practice.

🎧 **5.1 Listen again and practise saying the words and sentences. Pay attention in particular to the groups of consonants.**

Connected speech

B 🎧 **5.2 Listen to the pronunciation of *has / have* and *hasn't / haven't* in the sentences.**

/z/
1 She's completely changed her lifestyle.

/ˈhæznt/
2 He hasn't seen a stress counsellor yet.

/v/
3 They've appointed a new management team.

/ˈhævnt/
4 They haven't introduced flexitime yet.

C 🎧 **5.3 Listen to the recording and complete the sentences.**

1 .... never made a presentation.
2 .... never travelled abroad.
3 .... gone on a training course.
4 .... been under a lot of stress.
5 .... taken time off work this year.
6 .... finished our report.

🎧 **5.3 Listen again and practise saying the sentences. Pay attention to the contractions.**

Stress and intonation

D 🎧 **5.4 Listen and complete the question tag in each of the sentences.**

1 They were overworked, ... they?
2 She's been under stress recently, ... she?
3 They weren't feeling relaxed, ... they?
4 You haven't missed the deadline, ... you?
5 He resigned last week, ... he?
6 She didn't come to work yesterday, ... she?

Sound work

Tip

In spoken English, you can use a question tag if you expect someone to agree with you. When you use such question tags, your voice goes down:

He hasn't finished yet, has he?

🎧 5.4 **Listen again and practise saying the sentences.**

Making and responding to suggestions

Ⓐ 🎧 5.5 **Listen to the recording and complete Speaker B's suggestions.**

a) B: _How about_ .... introducing flexitime?

b) B: .... make sure they don't have to work overtime more than once a week.

c) B: Well, ... you take it home with you and finish it over the weekend then.

d) B: .... call a meeting to discuss the problem, so we can look for ways of making them less strict?

e) B: .... asking your boss to stop putting them up?

f) B: Well, ... make it absolutely clear to everyone that only mobiles may be used for private conversations.

Ⓑ **Match Speaker A's problems with the suggestions a) – f) in exercise A.**

1 A: Employees who leave early have become a serious problem. ☐ d
2 A: I can't meet my sales targets. ☐
3 A: Everybody complains about the tight deadlines. ☐
4 A: I'm afraid I can't finish this report by Friday. ☐
5 A: Many of us need to make a personal call sometimes. ☐
6 A: Our admin staff all say they can't balance their work and home lives. ☐

Ⓒ 🎧 5.6 **Listen to suggestions 1 – 7 and match them with responses a) – g). You will hear each suggestion twice.**

a) Excellent idea! We could offer a full month to those who've been with us for over three years. ☐

b) I don't agree at all. They already have free membership of the sports centre. ☐

c) Maybe, but I think sending out a questionnaire would be more effective. ☐

d) Mm, good idea. Most of our employees have children. I'm sure they'd welcome the idea. ☐

e) Yes, I suppose that's worth considering. We'd certainly have a longer weekend. ☐ 1

f) I'm not sure I agree. In my view, there should be a smoking area on each floor. ☐

g) That sounds interesting, but I think varying the menus and offering healthier meals is more important. ☐

UNIT 6 — Entertaining

Individual sounds

A 🎧 **6.1 Listen to how the letters in bold are pronounced.**

> ~~theatre~~   change   programme   want   talk   starter

B Write the words from exercise A next to the key phrase which contains the same sound (see page 52).

1 a'bout 'Canada .....*theatre*.....
2 bad bank ....
3 play safe ....
4 short course ....
5 smart card ....
6 top job ....

C Put the words from the box into the correct column, according to the pronunciation of the letter(s) in bold.

> ~~access~~   company   large   target
> always   corporate   quality   thanks
> call   favourite   spacious   watch

/ə/ as in a'bout 'Canada	/æ/ as in bad bank	/eɪ/ as in play safe	/ɔː/ as in short course	/ɑː/ as in smart card	/ɒ/ as in top job
....	*access*	....	....	....	....
....	....	....	....	....	....

🎧 **6.2 Check your answers. Then listen again and practise saying the words.**

Connected speech

D 🎧 **6.3 Listen to the way certain words are linked in the sentences.**

1 She put‿off the meeting.
2 She put‿it‿off.
3 I looked‿up their‿address.
4 I looked‿it‿up.

What's the rule?
When a word finishes with a **consonant** and the word immediately after begins with a **vowel** sound, we usually link those two words.

🎧 **6.3 Listen again and practise saying the sentences.**

E Indicate where similar links could be made in these sentences.

1 Several extra visitors turned up.
2 They took up our invitation.
3 She took us out to an excellent restaurant.
4 We should set up online sales as soon as we can.

🎧 **6.4 Check your answers. Then listen again and practise saying the sentences.**

Making small talk

A Complete the excerpts from conversations with words from the box. You will not need all the words.

~~have~~	afraid	Can	do	please	How	meet	like
Nice	see	thanks	know	would	did	thank	What

1 A: David, ...*have*......... you met Elisa Vasconcelos?
   B: No. Hello, Elisa. Nice to .... you.

2 A: Jameel, do you .... Sylvia?
   B: Yes, of course. Hi Sylvia, good to .... you again.

3 A: How do you .... My name's Joko Hartono.
   B: .... to meet you. Mine's Brendan Lenehan.

4 A: .... are things?
   B: Fine .... It's good to be here.

5 A: .... I get you something to drink?
   B: That .... be nice. Thanks. I'll have some fruit juice.

🎧 **6.5 Listen and check your answers. Then listen again and practise B's part.**

B 🎧 **6.6 Listen and tick the most appropriate response a), b) or c) for each item that you hear.**

1 a) How about you?
  b) Yeah. Just a little delay.
  c) Yes. I'm on the first flight to Paris tomorrow.

2 a) It's great. And just a five-minute walk from here.
  b) It's 502-2798.
  c) Yes. There're two excellent hotels in the Old Town.

3 a) Never again, thank you very much.
  b) Well, I never.
  c) Just once. I attended a conference here two years ago.

4 a) Yes, please.
  b) Help yourself to some food.
  c) As long as I stick to the city centre, I'm fine.

5 a) Till the end of the conference.
  b) At the Palace Hotel.
  c) Yes, quite a long time, in fact.

6 a) Sure. It's 233-2453.
  b) Yes, of course. Just go ahead.
  c) E-mailing is much faster.

C 🎧 **6.7 Listen to conversation openings 1 – 7 and match them to the responses a) – g).**

a) Did you? Were you based in Kuala Lumpur? ☐
b) Mm. Is that one of the martial arts? ☐
c) So do you work in a laboratory? ☐
d) What a coincidence! And what sort of music does she like? ☐
e) You must be exhausted! Why didn't you fly? ☑
f) Really! That's one of the largest cities in Poland, isn't it? ☐
g) I'm glad you like it. And what's your favourite dish? ☐

Tip

Responding with just one or two words usually is not enough for a successful conversation. To show interest and keep the conversation going, make a comment or ask a question related to the topic, as in examples a) – g).

65

UNIT 7 — Marketing

Individual sounds

A 🎧 **7.1 Listen carefully to how the letters in bold are pronounced.**

/ɒ/ as in t**o**p j**o**b: l**o**ss   sh**o**p   wh**a**t

/ɔː/ as in sh**or**t c**our**se: l**au**nch   st**o**re   c**augh**t

B **Put the words from the box into the correct column, according to the pronunciation of the letter(s) in bold.**

c**or**porate   m**o**del   pr**o**duct   qu**a**lity   w**a**nt   c**our**se   f**ore**cast

/ɒ/ as in t**o**p j**o**b	/ɔː/ as in sh**or**t c**our**se

🎧 **7.2 Listen and check your answers. Then listen again and practise saying the words.**

Connected speech

C 🎧 **7.3 Listen to how the words in *italics* are pronounced in these questions from a customer survey.**

- Which age group *do you* belong to?
- How much *did you* spend on soft drinks last month?
- *Would you* consider buying a different brand?

Tip

In informal speech, *do you* is often pronounced /djə/ or /djʊ/. *Did you* and *Would you* are often pronounced /'dɪdjə/, /'dɪdjʊ/ or /'wʊdjə/, /'wʊdjʊ/.

🎧 **7.3 Listen again and practise asking the questions.**

D 🎧 **7.4 Listen to the recording and complete the questions.**

1 . . . . take the packaging into account?
2 How often . . . . buy spring water?
3 How many bottles of water . . . . buy last week?
4 . . . . try fruit-flavoured mineral water?
5 What kind of soft drinks . . . . usually buy?

🎧 **7.4 Listen again and practise asking the questions.**

Stress and intonation

E 🎧 **7.5 Listen and mark whether all three words are stressed on the same syllable(✔) or not (✗).**

1 prod.uct ord.er serv.ice	✓
2 cred.it pay.ment suc.cess	✗
3 cam.paign fore.cast fig.ures	
4 qual.it.y pack.ag.ing mark.et.ing	
5 cust.om.er de.part.ment spec.ial.ist	

🎧 **7.5 Listen again and practise saying the words.**

Sound work

Using stress to correct information

A 🎧 **7.6 Listen to the telephone conversations. Notice how Speaker B uses stress to correct Speaker A.**

1 A: … and your agent in Uruguay is Juan José Buaro. B-U-A-R-O …
   B: Sorry, no. B-U-<u>E</u>-R-O.

2 A: All right. See you on Tuesday, then.
   B: Hold on a minute. The meeting is on <u>Thurs</u>day.

B **Look at the telephone conversations. Underline the part that Speaker B will stress to correct Speaker A.**

1 A: Ah, hello, Miss Peterson.
   B: Hello, Mr Gallegos. It's <u>Mrs</u> Peterson, actually. How can I help you?

2 A: … and my sales report will be with you by the thirtieth.
   B: Sorry, Ranesh. We're talking about the thirteenth.

3 A: So their number is 020 8224 7895.
   B: No, 8224 6895.

4 A: … and you said the advertising agency was at 75 Birchington Street.
   B: Well, it's Birchington Road, actually.

5 A: Good to hear you increased your market share by 9.5%.
   B: Sorry – I said 5.5%.

6 A: I hear 40% of the people you interviewed had difficulty finding our products.
   B: That's not quite right, I'm afraid. I said 14%.

🎧 **7.7 Listen to the recording and check your answers. Then listen again and practise Speaker B's replies.**

Getting the message right

C 🎧 **7.8 Listen to how Speaker B asks for the unclear piece of information to be repeated.**

1 A: We interviewed more than ***** people.
   B: Sorry, how many people did you interview?

2 A: ***** is unhappy about our sales figures.
   B: The line's very bad, I'm afraid. Who's unhappy about our sales figures?

D **Ask Speaker B to repeat the missing information in each of the statements.**

1 A: So our new hair conditioner will be launched on *****.
   B: I couldn't hear you. .... ?

2 A: We've already spent ***** on advertising.
   B: Sorry? .... ?

3 A: The ***** Manager was really very pleased.
   B: Sorry, ... ?

4 A: He'd like to meet you on ***** in the afternoon.
   B: It's a very bad line. .... ?

5 A: Our new range of toiletries should be targeted at *****.
   B: Sorry? .... ?

6 A: Our total sales were over *****.
   B: Sorry, ... ?

🎧 **7.9 Listen to the sample answers and practise Speaker B's responses.**

Survival business English

UNIT 8 — Planning

Individual sounds

A 🎧 **8.1 Listen to how the letters in bold are pronounced in the following words.**

> ~~holiday~~ do information ordinary other overspend work

B **Put the words from exercise A into the correct column, according to the pronunciation of the letters in bold.**

/ɒ/ as in top job	/ɔː/ as in short course	/uː/ as in school rules	/ʌ/ as in much luck	/ɜː/ as in first term	/ə/ as in a'bout 'Canada	/əʊ/ as in go slow
....holiday....	....	....	....	....	....	....
....	....	....	....	....	....	....

C **Put the words from the box into the correct column in exercise B, according to the pronunciation of the letters in bold.**

> office company forecast move open period world

🎧 **8.2 Check your answers. Then listen again and practise saying the words.**

Connected speech

D 🎧 **8.3 Listen to the pronunciation of *to* in these sentences.**
1   They expect to make a huge profit.
2   They're going to relaunch the series very soon.
3   They're hoping to attract foreign investors.

What's the rule?
- Before a consonant sound (1 and 2), *to* is often pronounced /tə/.
- Before a vowel sound (3), *to* is often pronounced /tʊ/.

E **Practise saying the sentences.**
1   What are you going to do?
2   They intend to expand in Poland.
3   He's planning to take early retirement.
4   We're hoping to open a subsidiary in Madrid.
5   They're going to do some research on their new product.

🎧 **8.4 Listen to the recording and 'shadow' (see page 53) the sentences.**

Stress and intonation

F **For each of the verbs, write the corresponding noun ending in *-tion* or *-sion*.**

1 inform	*information*	7 expand	....
2 implement	....	8 expect	....
3 prepare	....	9 modernise	....
4 consider	....	10 discuss	....
5 celebrate	....	11 decide	....
6 renovate	....	12 revise	....

🎧 **8.5 Listen to the recording and underline the stressed syllable in each verb and noun.**
Listen again and practise saying the words.

Sound work

Checking information

A Match the statements on the left with the appropriate request for clarification on the right.

1 A: We forecast an increase in sales.

2 A: I don't think I can finish my report by Wednesday.

3 A: Unfortunately, they did not estimate the costs properly.

4 A: I hope Peterson will attend the board meeting.

5 A: They're not expecting to move into their new offices until January.

6 A: It seems that there's going to be a slight delay.

a) B: You mean, it was a lot more expensive?

b) B: So what you're saying is that they are not sticking to their plan.

c) B: What exactly do you mean by 'slight delay'?

d) B: Are you saying that business is picking up, then?

e) B: You mean, you're not completely sure he'll come?

f) B: So what you're saying is that you won't be able to meet the deadline.

🎧 **8.6 Listen to the recording and check your answers. Then listen again and practise Speaker B's responses.**

B A secretary from Lindcom Hungary is calling Ana, the Sales Manager. Complete the conversation with the sentences from the box.

Kati: Ana?

Ana: ......*Yes. Speaking.*.. ¹.

Kati: Hi. I'm phoning about our visitors from Stockholm. I'm afraid they've changed their plans.

Ana: .... ².

Kati: Yes, they are. But they're arriving on Thursday, not on Wednesday as they originally planned.

Ana: .... ³.

Kati: Well, I think they're going to be very busy all day Thursday. You know, the Performance Evaluations and all that. They could see you after that, but I'm sure Friday morning would be better. Would 10 o'clock be convenient for you?

Ana: .... ⁴.

Kati: How about earlier, say 8.30?

Ana: .... ⁵.

Kati: Fine. I'll confirm the appointment as soon as possible.

Ana: .... ⁶.

a) I see. So what about our meeting?

b) All right. Let's make it 8 o'clock, just to be on the safe side.

c) Well, I'm seeing an important client at 10.15. I can't change that, I'm afraid.

d) Thanks, Kati. That's great.

e) ~~Yes. Speaking.~~

f) You mean, they're not coming next week?

🎧 **8.7 Listen and check your answers.**

C Underline all the forms in exercise B which are used to talk about the future.

Survival business English

UNIT 9 — Managing people

Individual sounds

A Make four groups of words with the same sounds.

> training approach persuasive goal number order
> other report shareholder talk trust pay

1 sales .....*training*..... ....
2 launch ....
3 money ....
4 flow ....

🎧 **9.1** Listen to the recording and check your answers. Then listen again and practise saying the words.

Connected speech

B 🎧 **9.2** Listen to the way certain words are linked in these sentences.

1 They told‿every one‿of‿us.
2 She finds‿it‿easy to delegate‿authority.
3 He believes‿in his‿employees'‿abilities.
4 They've‿invested‿a lot‿in training courses.
5 She likes to communicate‿information‿as‿often‿as possible.

What's the rule?
When a word finishes with a **consonant** and the word immediately after begins with a **vowel** sound, we usually link those two words.

🎧 **9.2** Listen again and practise saying the sentences.

C Show where similar links could be made in these sentences.
1 He gained a lot of experience abroad.
2 She told us that Alan wouldn't agree.
3 The department isn't investing enough in training.

🎧 **9.3** Listen to the recording and check your answers. Then listen again and practise saying the sentences.

Stress and intonation

D Put the words from the box in the correct column according to their stress pattern.

> budget mistake shareholder suggestion assistant
> consultant deputy invoice manager support

O o	o O	O o o	o O o
budget	*mistake*	*shareholder*	*suggestion*
....	....	....	....
		....	....

🎧 **9.4** Listen and check your answers. Then listen again and practise saying the words.

Sound work

Socialising

A Complete the sentences used when people say goodbye.

1 Keep ....*in*...... touch.
2 We'll .... in touch soon.
3 .... a safe journey back.
4 I hope we'll see you .... soon.
5 Thanks for looking .... me so well.
6 Thanks ever so much .... your hospitality.

🎧 **9.5 Listen and check your answers.**

B Match each question with the appropriate reply.

1 What do you usually do after work?
2 Any plans for this evening?
3 What do people here usually do at weekends?
4 We're going out. Why don't you join us?
5 How do you usually spend the summer?
6 So what do you think of Copenhagen?

a) It's great. Thanks for showing me around.
b) That's very kind of you, but some other time.
c) Well, I'd just like to stay in the hotel and relax.
d) We all go to see my parents in Toulouse.
e) Not much. I sometimes watch a video.
f) Many people go to their holiday cottages in the hills.

🎧 **9.6 Listen and check your answers. Then listen again and practise the responses.**

C 🎧 **9.7 Listen and tick the most appropriate response a), b) or c) for each item that you hear.**

1 a) I really enjoyed the meal.
  b) I hope we meet again soon. It's been great to be here.
  c) People always say that to me.

2 a) That was really hard work, wasn't it?
  b) I've enjoyed it too. Thank you.
  c) Yes, I like pleasure too.

3 a) Goodbye! Keep in touch!
  b) And even better to you.
  c) No, you're the best.

4 a) Not at all. Now it's your turn to invite us.
  b) Many happy returns!
  c) You're welcome. It's been great to have you with us.

5 a) It's very kind of you, but perhaps some other time.
  b) It's Saturday afternoon already.
  c) Thanks. Same to you.

Taking a message

D 🎧 **9.8 Your colleague is away and has asked you to check their voice mail. Listen to each message 1 – 4. Note down who rang and what was said or asked. Then write a short note for your colleague, as in the example.**

> Max called about your presentation on Friday. He asked what time you wanted to start. He also asked if the boardroom was OK.

Survival business English

UNIT 10   Conflict

Individual sounds

A 🎧 **10.1 Listen to the *schwa* sound (/ə/) in these words (see page 52).**

O o	o O	o O o	O o o
patient nervous	propose success	behaviour consistent	compromise sympathy

Tip

Notice that non-stressed syllables often have a schwa sound (/ə/).

🎧 **10.1 Listen again and practise saying the words.**

B **In each word, underline the letter(s) pronounced /ə/.**

advice	solution	company	complaint	customer	entertainment

🎧 **10.2 Listen to the recording and check your answers. Then listen again and practise saying the words.**

Connected speech

C 🎧 **10.3 Listen to how the forms in bold are spoken.**

We **won't** pay.	I**'ll** do it.
We**'ll** see.	I**'d** agree.
We **wouldn't** answer.	She**'ll** send it.
We**'d** complain.	She**'d** sign it.

D 🎧 **10.4 Listen and complete the sentences with *'ll, won't, 'd* or *wouldn't*.**

1 I . . . . resign immediately.
2 I . . . . send them a fax.
3 We . . . . deliver the goods this week.
4 They . . . . close our account.
5 We . . . . reduce the price.
6 We . . . . pay all transport costs.
7 They . . . . pay you a higher commission.
8 We . . . . sign the contract.

🎧 **10.4 Listen and check your answers. Then listen again and practise saying the sentences.**

Stress and intonation

E 🎧 **10.5 As you listen to the recording, match the sentence halves.**

↗	↘
1 If we pay late,	a) they'll give you a bonus.
2 If you delivered this week,	b) we'll give you an extra discount.
3 If you gave us a 10% discount,	c) they'll close our account.
4 If you exceed the sales target,	d) we'd pay all transport costs.
5 If you pay cash,	e) we'd place our order early next week.

Tip

Notice the rising intonation at the end of the first part, and the falling intonation at the end of the second part.

🎧 **10.5 Listen again and practise saying the sentences.**

Dealing with conflict

A 🎧 **10.6 Listen to five people talking about various conflict situations. Decide what the conflict was about.**

- Write one letter, **a) – g)**, next to the number of the speaker.
- Do not use any letter more than once.

Speaker 1 . . . .

Speaker 2 . . . .

Speaker 3 . . . .

Speaker 4 . . . .

Speaker 5 . . . .

a) a misunderstanding about a deadline

b) a personality clash between colleagues

c) a team leader unhappy about the schedule

d) an e-mail sent to the wrong person

e) a buyer and a seller disagreeing about some of the terms of a deal

f) staff and manager unable to work together

g) staff unhappy about extra administrative work

B 🎧 **10.6 Listen again and decide what the consequence of each conflict was.**

- Write one letter, **a) – g)**, next to the number of the speaker.
- Do not use any letter more than once.

Speaker 1 . . . .

Speaker 2 . . . .

Speaker 3 . . . .

Speaker 4 . . . .

Speaker 5 . . . .

a) nobody agreed to work part-time

b) the company decided to employ more staff

c) the employee asked to work in a different group

d) the manager left the company

e) somebody apologised

f) the company cancelled the order

g) some employees resigned

C 🎧 **10.7 Listen and complete the telephone conversation.**

A: Phillip's Office Supplies International. Good morning.

B: It's Mary Li here, from Sun Sing Advertising.

A: Hello, Ms Li. How can I ..... *help* .... ?

B: I'd like to make a complaint.

A: What seems to .... ?

B: You have just sent us the wrong invoice, I'm afraid.

A: Can you give me the details, please?

B: Right. The invoice number is 202.A and the order number you quote is BG/505. In fact, our order number is BG/503.

A: Now, let me see ... I'm .... It's our fault entirely.

I'm afraid there's been a mix-up.

B: When do you think you .... sort .... ?

A: I'll .... and call you back as soon as possible.

B: Thank you.

A: Don't .... Goodbye, Ms Li.

🎧 **10.7 Listen and practise Speaker B's part.**

Survival business English

UNIT 11 — New business

Individual sounds

A 🎧 **11.1 Listen to the difference between /ɒ/ and /ɔː/.**

/ɒ/	/ɔː/
n**o**t	n**ough**t
sp**o**t	sp**or**t
sh**o**t	sh**or**t

B **Underline all the letters that are pronounced /ɔː/ in these sentences.**

1 We'll send them <u>a</u>ll on a training course.
2 Let's sort out this problem before Pauline gets here.
3 According to this report, interest rates will soon fall.
4 We need to reform our tax system in order to stimulate exports.
5 They've closed 40 of their stores and cut their workforce by a quarter.

🎧 **11.2 Listen and check your answers. Then listen again and practise saying the sentences.**

> **Tip**
>
> To improve your pronunciation, getting the difference between long and short vowels is one of the most important things. So, make sure your long vowels are really long.
>
> *(See also Unit 1, exercises A and B.)*

Connected speech

C 🎧 **11.3 Listen to the way certain words are linked in these sentences.**

1 As soon‿as‿interest rates fall, consumer spending goes‿up.
2 I'll sign the new contract‿as soon‿as‿I've read‿all the details.

What's the rule?
When a word finishes with a **consonant** and the word immediately after begins with a **vowel** sound, we usually link those two words.

D **Show where similar links could be made in these sentences.**

1 We'll set up in that area when the situation has improved.
2 We'll sort it out when Allan arrives.

🎧 **11.4 Listen to the recording and check your answers. Then listen again and practise saying each sentence.**

Stress and intonation

E 🎧 **11.5 Listen to how the dates are spoken. Notice the main stresses in bold.**

1 January 20   **Ja**nuary the **twen**tieth
2 12 October   the **twelfth** of Oc**to**ber

F **Write the dates in full.**

1 14 Feb ....
2 Sept. 15 ....
3 16 April ....
4 Dec. 17 ....
5 3 June ....
6 4 July ....

🎧 **11.6 Listen and check your answers. Then listen again and underline the two stressed syllables you hear in each date.**

Numbers

A 🎧 **11.7 Listen to the recording and circle the numbers you hear.**

1	£13	£30	**5**	$18,000	$80,000
2	14%	40%	**6**	€1,200	€12,000
3	350 million	315 million	**7**	2/5	2.5
4	¥1,416	¥1,460			

🎧 **11.7 Listen again and practise saying the numbers.**

B **Match the questions to the answers.**

1   Did the unemployment rate decrease?

2   Do you know the Footsie index? [1]

3   What's the basic rate of income tax in the UK?

4   And what percentage of all income taxpayers pay the basic rate?

5   What's the euro – dollar exchange rate?

6   What's the population of the UK?

a) About 75 or 80%, I think.

b) Hold on … Yes. It closed 114.2 points higher at 5,833.9 points.

c) Mmm, somewhere between 0.79 and 0.82 against the dollar, I'd say.

d) Just over 60.5 million. So that's about 250 people per square kilometer.

e) Well, it was reduced from 23 to 22% a couple of years ago.

f) Yes. It went down by 0.5% to reach 11.3%.

[1] Footsie: the Financial Times Stock Exchange 100 Index; the main measure of the amount by which the leading 100 shares sold on the London Stock Exchange have gone up or down in value. It is brought up to date every minute of the working day.

🎧 **11.8 Listen and check your answers. Then listen and practise saying the sentences.**

C 🎧 **11.9 Listen to the economic profile and complete the table with the numbers you hear.**

THE COUNTRY IN FIGURES	
Growth rate: .... %	Agriculture: .... %
GDP per capita: $	Unemployment rate: .... %
Inflation rate:	
Labour force: .... million	**Budget**
Services: .... %	Revenues: $ .... billion
Industry: .... %	Expenditure: $ .... billion

D 🎧 **11.10 Listen to how Speaker A corrects Speaker B.**

1   A: Was that 2.5%?   2   A: Did you say 2.4%?
    B: No. 2.<u>8</u>%.   B: Sorry, no. <u>3</u>.4%.

E **Read the conversations and underline the numbers that Speaker B will stress.**

1   A: So the unemployment rate went up by 1.2%.
    B: Sorry, no, I said 1.1%.

2   A: So, 36.7% of the people in Denmark own a computer.
    B: 37.7%, to be precise.

3   A: Did you say the GDP totalled £853 billion last year?
    B: Not quite. It was £843 billion.

🎧 **11.11 Listen and check your answers. Then listen again and practise Speaker B's part.**

Survival business English

UNIT 12   Products

A 🎧 **12.1 Listen and add the missing letters in the words.**

1   _s t_ylish; _ _ow; _ _oduce
2   co_ _ _ _ _able; manufa_ _ure
3   Our new _ _odu_ _ _ are a_ _ _a_ _ive and _ _a_ _ical.
4   They're also _ _exi_ _ _ and user-_ _ien_ _y.
5   We have a lot of products for cu_ _omers with busy li_ _ _ _yles.
6   They ha_ _ _'_ annou_ _ _ _ the lau_ _ _ date yet.

> **Tip**
>
> Many English words have groups of two, three or four consonant sounds pronounced together. Pronouncing those groups of consonants correctly often requires a lot of practice.

🎧 **12.1 Listen again and practise saying the words and sentences. Pay attention in particular to the groups of consonants.**

Connected speech

B **Complete the sentences with *Its*, *It has* or *It is*.**

1   _It is_ .... ideal for storing CDs.
2   .... got lots of interesting features.
3   .... weight is just under 3 kilos.
4   .... most attractive feature is that .... easy to operate.
5   .... got all you need for home and office use.
6   .... available in three different colours.

Check your answers.

🎧 **12.2 Then listen and practise saying the sentences. Use the contractions (e.g., *it's*), as in the recording.**

Stress and intonation

C 🎧 **12.3 Listen and complete items 1 – 8.**

1   _It's_ .... de<u>li</u>vered ...
2   .... manu<u>fac</u>tured ...
3   .... <u>mo</u>dified ...
4   .... discon<u>tin</u>ued ...
5   .... <u>ad</u>vertised ...
6   .... pro<u>mo</u>ted ...
7   .... <u>tes</u>ted ...
8   .... in<u>sur</u>ed ...

> **Tips**
>
> • Notice the contractions, e.g., *they have been* is pronounced /ðeɪvbɪn/.
>
> • Notice the weak forms, e.g., /ə/ for *are*, /wə/ for *were*.
>
> • Notice the stress on the verbs, e.g., de<u>li</u>vered, discon<u>tin</u>ued.

🎧 **12.3 Listen again and practise saying items 1 – 8.**

D 🎧 **12.4 Listen and match the sentence endings a) – h) with the items from exercise C.**

a) ... after the tests.　　　3

b) ... against fire.　　　8

c) ... in all national newspapers.　☐

d) ... to senior managers.　☐

e) ... because of poor sales.　☐

f) ... in Korea.　☐

g) ... in our laboratories.　☐

h) ... within a week.　☐

🎧 **12.4 Listen again and practise saying the sentences.**

Asking questions about a product

A 🎧 **12.5 Listen and tick the most appropriate response a), b) or c) for each item that you hear.**

1　a)　Yes, I could.

　　b)　Well, we are expert furniture makers.

　　c)　Sure. To start with, it's made of the finest wood.

2　a)　It comes in three shades of brown, each with a matt or gloss finish.

　　b)　I'm afraid it's not available this year.

　　c)　We are very interested in colours, but ask me about the price, too.

3　a)　The special screen gives excellent images.

　　b)　Without battery, it's just under 250g.

　　c)　As I said, you can hold it in the palm of your hand.

4　a)　No, I said it did.

　　b)　Yes. It is the most economical on the market.

　　c)　I talked about a lot of devices.

5　a)　I agree. Absolutely unique.

　　b)　It will be sold everywhere.

　　c)　Its small size and its beautiful design.

6　a)　There's a 12-month basic guarantee on all our products.

　　b)　Of course. We always do.

　　c)　Everything is still under guarantee.

Presenting a product

B **Complete the text with words from the box.**

> ~~features~~　appeal　advantage　stylish　costs
> weighs　value　ideal　steel　length

- Our new model has several special . *features* which will .... to our customers.
- It's ...., and it's made of stainless ....
- It .... just under 2.2 kilos, and its .... is 21 centimeters.
- It's .... for the office.
- Another .... is that it's very user friendly.
- And finally, it .... 99 euros – great .... for money.

🎧 **12.6 Listen to the presentation and check your answers.**

C 🎧 **12.7 Listen to excerpts from six presentations. Match the excerpts to the products a) – f).**

a) a burglar alarm　☐

b) a coffee machine　1

c) an executive briefcase　☐

d) a printer　☐

e) an air-conditioner　☐

f) a watch　☐

Survival business English

Answer key

Language work

1 Careers

Vocabulary

A

2 b   3 a   4 b   5 a   6 c   7 c   8 a   9 a

B

2 looks
3 deals
4 is responsible
5 is in charge
6 makes sure

C

1 d   2 e   3 a   4 c   5 b

Language review

A

2 let
3 moving
4 start
5 contact
6 sharing
7 send

B

b 4   c 5   d 7   e 6   f 1   g 2

C

1 could   3 could   5 was able to
2 was able to 4 was able to

Writing

A

2 Telephone   6 Special skills   10 Interests
3 E-mail   7 Experience   11 Referees
4 Profile   8 Qualifications
5 Achievements   9 Personal details

B

2 5   3 6   4 10   5 4

C Sample answer

> Dear Sir or Madam,
>
> With reference to your advertisement in *The Hastings Herald* of 25 June, I would like to apply for the position of Communications Assistant.
>
> I feel I am well qualified for the position as I have A-levels in Social Sciences and Literature. As for my personal qualities, I am outgoing and like meeting new people.
>
> Please let me know if you require any further information.
>
> I look forward to hearing from you.
>
> Yours faithfully,

D

2 employs *not* employ   5 questions *not* question
3 keep *not* keeping   6 in *not* for
4 than *not* then

2 Selling online

Vocabulary

A

1 a bargain   4 to purchase
2 a warehouse   5 to refund
3 to despatch / to dispatch

B

2 f   3 e   4 b   5 a   6 d

C

2 order   4 turnover
3 refund   5 despatch

D

2 a   3 c   4 c   5 a   6 c   7 b   8 b

Language review

A

1 b   2 c   3 d   4 a

B

2 should despatch orders quickly.
3 don't have to (don't need to) register.
4 should put your logo on every page of your site.
5 don't have to (don't need to) pay until July.
6 mustn't make any mistakes!

C

2 e   3 a   4 d   5 f   6 b

D

Past: had to; didn't need to
Present: don't have to; mustn't forget
Future: we'll have to; won't have to

Writing

A

2 b   3 e   4 c   5 a   6 g   7 d   8 f   9 h   10 i

B

1 Dear   4 goods
2 Thank you   5 We look forward to doing
3 We confirm   6 Yours sincerely

C

1 placing   3 deliver   5 doing
2 receipt   4 hesitate

D

3 a   6 to   9 to
4 ✓   7 and
5 they   8 ✓

3 Companies

Vocabulary

A

2 f   3 d   4 c   5 g   6 b   7 a

B

2 a   3 b   4 c   5 a   6 c   7 b

C

1 Research and development (R&D)
2 Accounts
3 Administration (Admin)
4 Human resources (HR/Personnel)
5 Sales and marketing

Language review

A

2 a   3 c   4 b   5 f   6 d

B

1 Our company *is looking* for a new Marketing Manager.
5 This year, all our sales staff *are learning* French.
6 At the moment, we *do not know* the profit figures.

C

2 has   6 is attending
3 travels (*or* goes) 7 is thinking
4 is going (*or* is travelling) 8 knows
5 speaks (*or* knows) 9 is preparing

D Sample answers

2 How many countries does Kayavis have distributors in?
3 When is Sofia going to Canada?
4 Why is she going to Canada?
5 What foreign languages does she speak?
6 Why is she learning German?/Why is she attending a German course?
7 Where is the owner of Kayavis thinking of opening a shop and a large restaurant?

Writing

A

a 4   b 7   c 5   d 2   e 1   f 6   g 3   h 8

B Sample answer

> Thanks for the draft agenda of our forthcoming meeting.
>
> It seems fine to me. However, I think we should also discuss setting up online sales.
>
> Increasing sales and profits is extremely important for our company, and going online is probably the best way to achieve that.
>
> I too look forward very much to seeing you soon.
>
> Kind regards,

C Sample answers

3 ✓
4 ✓
5 them *not* they
6 ✓
7 attaching *not* attach
8 suggestions *not* suggestion
9 ✓
10 apologies *not* apologise

D

2 because
3 but
4 so
5 because
6 but
7 so
8 because
9 so
10 because

4 Great ideas

Vocabulary

2 d   3 f   4 e   5 b   6 a

2 protecting the environment
3 addresses a need
4 developing a business idea
5 reduce waste
6 made money

2 a   3 b   4 a   5 c   6 b   7 b   8 a   9 c

Language review

2 d   3 e   4 f   5 b   6 a

4 The agency *did not believe* that the machine would save so much time.
5 Zirkon *was already making* good profits when it introduced its new digital camera in 2000.
6 The story goes that *he had* the idea for the electric shoebrush while he was washing up.

1 **b** launched	**c** rocketed	**d** improved
2 **e** decided	**f** was working	**g** was touring
h developed	**i** took	**j** believed
3 **k** were planning	**l** waited	**m** was selling

Writing

b 3   c 6   d 5   e 4   f 2

B Sample answer

> On Sunday, the International Exhibition is open from 10am to 6pm.
> The admission charge for groups of 10 or more is 8 francs.
> The official catalogue is published in French and English only.

C Sample answer

> At the International Exhibition of Inventions, New Techniques and Products last Sunday, I saw a new type of confidential shredder which I think would save us a lot of time and money.
>
> The machine shreds both paper and cardboard and is fully automatic. It is also very quiet.
>
> I think it would be a very good investment as it would be more economical in the long run than using the services of a specialist firm.
>
> You can get more information from their website on www.safe-shreds.com.

D

3 the   6 they   9 ✓
4 ✓   7 and   10 for
5 was   8 never

5 Stress

Vocabulary

2 a   3 b   4 b   5 a   6 c   7 c   8 a   9 c   10 b   11 b

B

1 in / to
2 of / in
3 of
4 In / in / in / of / in
5 to
6 to / of
7 of / to

Language review

A

3 Yes, she has.   6 Yes, they have.
4 No, she hasn't.   7 Yes, Sergio has.
5 No, they haven't.

B Sample answers

3 Has Paola ever dealt with an aggressive customer?
4 Has Tim ever dealt with an aggressive customer?
5 Have Tim and Mark ever suffered from jet-lag?
6 Has Paola ever suffered from jet-lag?

C

2 's been (has been)
3 haven't had (have not had)
4 expected
5 thought
6 have been
7 had to
8 was
9 offered
10 needed
11 saved
12 've worked (have worked)
13 've never felt (have never felt)

Writing

  Sample answer

> According to a recent survey, over 14% of all employed people in the EU suffer from stress. Two of the main reasons are overwork and fear of redundancies. In addition, a large number of employees are suffering from headaches, backache and chest pains because of overcrowded offices, poor ventilation and badly designed furniture and equipment. Over the last few years(,) this has resulted in increased levels of absenteeism and a gradual decrease in productivity.

B

2a However, more men than women suffer from stress-related illnesses.

  b That is because their coping strategies are not as good as women's.

3a These pressures come from home and from work.

  b By contrast, many men are only under pressure at work.

4a To begin with, women are much more flexible than men.

  b Also, they usually cope with the pressures better than men.

 C

b 4   **c** 3   **d** 2

 D

2 showed	**5** have risen	**8** went up
3 increased	**6** has fallen	**9** stands
4 have made/are making	**7** stands	

The order is: b 5   **c** 6   **d** 2   **e** 4   **f** 3

E Sample answer

> I'm very sorry I won't be able to attend the seminar tomorrow morning. I need to stay at home for a couple of days because I can't shake off these terrible headaches. Moreover, I feel exhausted because I haven't slept well for a whole week.
>
> These are probably symptoms of stress, so I will see my doctor and perhaps a stress counsellor as well.
>
> I'll be back in my office on Wednesday morning.

F

2 absence *not* absent   **5** better *not* best

3 are *not* is   **6** general *not* generally

4 leads *not* leading

6 Entertaining

Vocabulary

 A

2 guest	**7** wide	**12** delicious
3 abroad	**8** dishes	**13** negotiate
4 stressful	**9** order	**14** dessert
5 aperitif	**10** starter	**15** bill
6 menu	**11** course	**16** manager

B

1 a   **2** c   **3** c   **4** b   **5** a

Language review

 A

2 b   **3** f   **4** g   **5** h   **6** d   **7** e   **8** a

 B

The order is: a 1   **b** 5   **c** 2   **d** 7   **e** 6   **f** 8(3)   **g** 4(8)
                h 3(4)

 C

3 if nobody turns **up** at the airport *not* if nobody turns in at the airport

5 come **up** with some suggestions *not* come around with some suggestions

 D

2 The doctor said I was overworked and advised me to *slow down*.

3 You have to respect your superiors, of course, but you also have to *stand up for* your opinions.

4 We *looked for* a new Sales Manager with at least three years' experience.

5 If you want to buy a new computer, it is a good idea to *shop about*.

6 At the time, the government was trying to encourage people to *set up* new businesses.

7 The company's owners have *set aside* € 500,000 to invest in their business.

Writing

 A

2 The most popular activity   **5** far less frequently

3 Secondly   **6** with a very small number

4 almost as many   **7** Finally

B

2 c   **3** a   **4** e   **5** b

C Sample answer

> Dear Jim,
>
> We've booked Robert Dorey for 2 nights (5th & 6th) into the Astoria. He will be in Room 507, which is on a non-smoking floor.
>
> The Astoria is a very comfortable four-star hotel just 5 minutes from the centre.
>
> Looking forward to Robert's visit.
>
> Best wishes,
>
> Brian

D Sample answer

> Dear Brian,
>
> This is to thank you for your hospitality during and after the conference.
>
> You gave me a lot of your time and made my visit very memorable. Walking round the Old Town in the evening was really fascinating. Besides, I thought the food in that Mediterranean restaurant where we had supper was just perfect.
>
> It was a great pleasure to meet you. If you come to Canada, I would like to return your kindness and generosity.
>
> Once again, thank you.
>
> Regards,
>
> Robert

Answer key: Language work

7 Marketing

Vocabulary

Across 1 share 5 free 6 need 7 cycle 9 aim 10 sales 11 sell
Down 2 agency 3 range 4 budget 5 figures 8 costs 9 ads

2 a 3 b 4 b 5 c 6 a 7 c 8 c

Language review

2 Why	5 Who	8 What
3 How much	6 Which	
4 How many	7 How long	

b 8 c 1 d 6 e 5 f 7 g 2 h 4

2 Would you like to talk to our Marketing Manager?
3 Do they spend a lot on advertising?
4 Where did they advertise their new range?
5 Did you meet your sales targets?
6 Were you expecting better sales figures?
7 Have you read my quarterly sales report?
8 How often do you write a report?

b 3 c 8 d 1 e 2 f 4 g 6 h 5

Writing

 Sample answer

Dear Mr Rijsbergen,

Many thanks for your enquiry of 2 June.

Please find enclosed our current catalogue, which contains detailed information about all our healthy food and drink products.

We also enclose a leaflet about *Fontaine*, our leading brand of spring water. *Fontaine* is a lightly sparkling natural spring water with no calories which offers real benefits.

We are particularly proud that the medical authorities of our country have already recommended it for consumption in hospitals and school restaurants.

Please let us know if you would like one of our representatives to visit you and present you with a sample of all our best-selling soft drinks.

We look forward to hearing from you.

With best wishes,

Denis Langlois

Marketing Manager

a 4 b 3 c 2 d 7 e 5 f 1 g 6

2 withdrawn
3 delay
4 regard
5 sure
6 available
7 retail

3 will	7 it	
4 the	8 and	
5 he	9 ✓	
6 ✓	10 on	

8 Planning

Vocabulary

1 a report	3 information
2 a schedule	4 a profit

1 to call	3 to implement
2 to decrease	4 to keep within

2 reschedule the meeting	4 do research
3 finished my sales report	5 stick to the budget

Language review

5 in four days' time	4 the day after tomorrow
1 in ten minutes	6 the week after next
7 in three weeks' time	3 tomorrow morning
8 next month	2 tonight
9 next year	

3 We intend to launch a new range next summer.
4 We hope to beat our competitors before long.
5 We expect to open three new subsidiaries before long.
6 We intend to open a new sales office in Bratislava.

 Sample answers

1 leaving for Geneva	3 giving a talk
2 coming back	4 preparing for a meeting

Writing

Introduce an explanation: That is why
Introduce an example: For instance
Make an additional point: In addition

B

2 In addition
3 That is why
4 In addition/For instance
5 That is why
6 For instance

C

2 have to
3 cannot
4 are leaving

5 has to
6 seeing

D Sample answer

> Unfortunately our guests from Stockholm cannot be with us on Wednesday 24. So the Performance Evaluation is on Thursday 10.30–12.30. We expect all members of the Sales team to be there. I'm sorry if these changes cause you any inconvenience.

E

2 make *not* made
3 visits *not* visit
4 customer *not* custom
5 useful *not* usefully
6 where *not* were
7 do *not* doing
8 learn *not* earn

9 Managing people

Vocabulary

A

2 delegate / to
3 deal / with

4 invest / in
5 Communicate / with

6 respond / to
7 believe / in

B

2 with / about
3 to / about
4 with / on
5 to / for / with
6 on / to

C

2 Socialising <u>with</u> colleagues is sometimes a good way to learn about what is happening in different departments.
3 Linda would like to discuss ~~about~~ the report's recommendations with you.
4 My company spends a lot of money <u>on</u> training courses for employees.
5 He may become a good manager. It depends <u>on</u> his communication skills.
6 ✓

Language review

A

2 I replied my computer wasn't working properly.
3 He said that I needed a new one.
4 Then he also said I should try to plan ahead.
5 I answered that I was usually well organised.
6 Finally, I asked him when I would get a new computer.

B

2 isn't working properly
3 need a new one
4 try to plan ahead

5 usually well organised
6 will I get a new computer

C

2 ✓
3 They asked him how he *dealt* with those problems in his previous job.
4 ✓
5 ✓
6 He *said* that last month's sales figures were very good. / He told *me* (*him/her/us*, etc.) that last month's sales figures were very good.

D

1 He asked her if she adapted easily to new situations.
2 He asked her how often she invested in courses.
3 He asked her if she was having difficulty contacting their consultant.
4 He asked her why this year's budget was so small.

Writing

A

2 94%
3 31%
4 100%

5 4%
6 48%
7 54%

8 0%

B

2 a quarter of
3 One-third

4 almost half
5 almost everybody

C

2 d   3 e   4 c   5 a

D

2 k   3 j   4 b   5 g   6 l   7 f

10 Conflict

Vocabulary

A

2 a   3 f   4 b   5 c   6 d

B

2 impatient
3 informal
4 irresponsible

5 uncooperative
6 impolite
7 unresponsive

8 unemotional
9 uncritical
10 inconsistent

C

2c informal   **4a** irresponsible   **6c** uncritical
3b uncooperative   **5b** inconsistent

Language review

A

2 c   **3** f   **4** e   **5** b   **6** a

B

2 they wouldn't
3 they will
4 No, they
5 (Yes,) I will
6 he wouldn't
7 we (or I) will

C

2 'd   **4** won't   **6** won't
3 'll   **5** wouldn't

D

2 paid   **6** will do/'ll do
3 deliver   **7** will cover/'ll cover
4 would deliver/'d deliver **8** ordered
5 increases

Writing

A

2 request   **4** invite
3 complain   **5** enquire

B

2 request   **4** invitation
3 complaint   **5** enquiry

C

a 5   **b** 3   **c** 6   **d** 1   **e** 4   **f** 2

D Sample answer

> Further to your phone call and your letter of 23 March, we would like to apologise for the problems you had.
>
> There was obviously a mix-up over your order, and the goods you received were meant for another customer. The correct order was sent by special delivery and should already be with you.
>
> Once again, our apologies for this inconvenience.
>
> We look forward to further orders from you.

E

2 place *not* placing   **6** to *not* on
3 do *not* did   **7** has *not* have
4 some *not* any   **8** as *not* like
5 cultural *not* culturally

11 New business

Vocabulary

A

2 unemployment rate   **7** balance of trade
3 exchange rate   **8** inflation rate
4 labour force   **9** foreign investment
5 government bureaucracy   **10** tax incentives
6 gross domestic product

B

2 a   **3** f   **4** e   **5** d   **6** c

C

1 subsidies   **2** foreign debt   **3** recession

Language review

A

2 ✓
3 ✓
4 We'll phone you when the goods are here.
5 ✓
6 ✓
7 We'll deal with insurance after they've told us about their special discount.
8 Our guests would like to visit the unit before they go back to Qatar.
9 ✓
10 ✓

B

2 d   **3** b   **4** a   **5** c   **6** g   **7** e

C Sample answers

2 I want to see Julia's report as soon as she's finished it. (*or* … as soon as she finishes it.)
3 I won't invite them until they've apologised. (*or* … until they apologise.)
4 Let's contact his referees before we employ him.
5 I'll give you a copy of the report when I've typed it up.
6 Read the contracts when you're on the plane.
7 Let's buy before prices increase.
8 As soon as we've won the contract, we'll inform our shareholders. (*or* As soon as we win the contract, …)

Writing

A

2 e   **3** f   **4** c   **5** b   **6** a

B Sample answers

2 The government is making exports easier in order to improve the balance of trade.
3 In order to stop companies polluting the air and the water, the government is passing a very strict environmental law.
4 The government is raising taxes in order to reduce the budget deficit.
5 In order to stimulate consumer spending, the government is lowering the interest rate.
6 The government is trying to reduce bureaucracy in order to attract foreign investors.

- On the other hand, around one in *six* men employed were in health, education and public administration services in 1995, while the same industry accounted for one-fifth of men's jobs in 2005.
- As regards the percentage of men employed in financial and business services, it increased from *ten* in 1995 to 15 *ten* years later.

 Sample answer

- One-fifth of all women employed were in manufacturing in 1995, compared with only one-tenth a decade later.
- On the other hand, 40% of women employees were in health, education, and public administration services in 1995, while this sector accounted for 45% of all women employed ten years later.
- As regards the percentage of women employed in financial and business services, it doubled from 1995 to 2005, when it accounted for one-fifth of women employed.

3 an	7 ✓	11 but
4 and	8 so	12 ✓
5 their	9 ✓	13 it
6 the	10 so	

12 Products

Vocabulary

1 popular	3 economical	5 fashionable
2 reliable	4 attractive	6 unique

2 hard-wearing	4 best-selling	6 well-made
3 high-tech	5 long-lasting	

C

2 custom-made	4 Downmarket
3 multi-purpose	5 First-class

D

2 b 3 a 4 c 5 a 6 c 7 b 8 b

Language review

A

2 f 3 d 4 e 5 a 6 b
Passive forms:

2 are made	5 will be modified
3 will be distributed	6 was launched
4 can be improved	

B

2 Your washing machine is being repaired now.
3 This new drug was developed by Bayer.
4 The effects of Alkaphen were still being researched into.
5 All selling rights have been retained by Bayer.
6 The question is, has our new range been promoted enough?

7 If sales continue to fall, it will have to be discontinued.
8 This new product should be tested immediately.
9 Its distribution could be improved.
10 The packaging definitely has to be improved.

2f In the future, a lot more shopping will be done online.
3b Nestlé food products are consumed by millions of people every day.
4c The 'little black dress' was created by Chanel, the French fashion designer.
5a The telephone was invented by A. G. Bell.
6e They claim that none of their new cosmetics are (*or* have been) tested on animals.

Writing

1 This new instant coffee has been produced by a well-known company *which (that)* has always sold its coffee in the higher price ranges.
2 The shop floor is an area in a factory *where* ordinary workers do their work.
3 A retailer is a person *who* owns or runs a shop selling goods to members of the public.
4 Sick leave is a period of time *when* you stay away from your job because you are ill.

2 run
3 high-performance
4 market leader
5 including
6 further information

C **Sample answer**

> Dear Sir/Madam,
>
> With reference to your advertisement in the September issue of *TechNews*, we would like to request further information about the Alpha JTX2.
>
> In particular, we need to know whether it can scan 3-D objects, and also what types of paper it takes.
>
> We are considering asking for a free trial. Could you tell us how long we would be able to keep the machine?
>
> Thank you in advance.
> Looking forward to hearing from you.
>
> Yours faithfully,

2 no *not* not
3 has *not* have
4 customers' *not* costumiers'
5 their *not* they
6 This *not* These

Talk business

Introduction

Vowels		
/ɒ/	/e/	/ɑː/
1 job	1 sell	1 card
2 knowledge	2 friendship	2 heart
3 want	3 said	3 laugh
/eɪ/	/eə/	/aɪ/
1 pay	1 share	1 price
2 break	2 chair	2 buyer
3 train	3 their	3 height
Consonants		
/ʃ/	/s/	/j/
1 option	1 sell	1 year
2 conscious	2 advice	2 Europe
3 insurance	3 scientific	3 million

1 Careers

Sound work

B *See audio script 1.2*

Survival business English

A *See audio script 1.6.*

B *See audio script 1.7.*

C *See audio script 1.8.*

D *See audio script 1.10.*

2 Selling online

Sound work

A

3 ✗   4 ✓   5 ✓   6 ✗

B

1 /aʊ/   2 /ə/   3 /æ/

C *See audio script 2.2.*

Survival business English

A *See audio script 2.4.*

B

1 we'll agree to that / that sounds reasonable
2 despatched / shipped
3 we'd prefer to pay / we'd rather pay
4 cover / be responsible for
Note: In this context, the phrases in each pair **mean the same.**

C *See audio script 2.5.*

3 Companies

Sound work

B

2 1 syllable   5 2 syllables   8 3 syllables
3 2 syllables   6 3 syllables
4 3 syllables   7 1 syllable

C *See audio script 3.3.*

E *See audio script 3.5.*

Survival business English

A *See audio script 3.6.*

B

2 retailers   7 190
3 age range   8 7.6
4 supply wholesale products   9 4%
5 top three   10 of teenage fashion
6 300   11 the leader

C Sample answer

Good afternoon, everyone. My name is Pierre Chevrel. I'm the general manager of *Espace Mode*. The purpose of this presentation is to give you some basic information about our company.

I'd like to start by saying where we are and what we do. We are situated in Grenoble, and we are manufacturers and retailers of clothes under the 'C-Kool' and 'Mirabelle' brand names.

Our customers are young men and women from all walks of life, in the age range 16–25. We also supply wholesale products to agents and mail order catalogues.

Now, I'd like to turn to our market position. We are among the French top three in the clothing sector. As regards our workforce, we employ almost 300 people.

If we can now look at our revenues, last year we achieved an annual turnover of over 190 million euros and generated profits of 7.6 million, that is to say 4% of sales.

Finally, a few words about our future plans. We are working on exciting new designs which will reflect a completely new concept of teenage fashion. I'm sure this will make *Espace Mode* the leader of the European fashion market.

4 Great ideas

Sound work

A

2 ✓   4 ✗   6 ✓
3 ✗   5 ✓

D

2 1 syllable	**5** 2 syllables	**8** 3 syllables
3 2 syllables	**6** 1 syllable	
4 3 syllables	**7** 1 syllable	

E *See audio script 4.4.*

Survival business English

A

Speaker 2: a
Speaker 3: d
Speaker 4: c
Speaker 5: b
Speaker 6: d
Speaker 7: c
Speaker 8: a

B *See audio script 4.6.*

C

The order is: **a** 2   **b** 4   **c** 3   **d** 7   **e** 5   **f** 1   **g** 6
1 a very special new product / a major new product
2 have to decide / have to agree
3 are not very happy / are not satisfied

5 Stress

Sound work

A *See audio script 5.1.*

C *See audio script 5.3.*

D *See audio script 5.4.*

Survival business English

A *See audio script 5.5.*

B

2 e   **3** d   **4** c   **5** f   **6** b

C

a 7   **b** 6   **c** 2   **d** 3   **e** 1   **f** 4   **g** 5

6 Entertaining

Sound work

B

2 programme
3 change
4 talk
5 starter
6 want

C *See audio script 6.2.*

E *See audio script 6.4.*

Survival business English

A *See audio script 6.5.*

B

1 b   **2** a   **3** c   **4** c   **5** a   **6** b

C

a 6   **b** 4   **c** 5   **d** 3   **e** 1   **f** 7   **g** 2

7 Marketing

Sound work

B *See audio script 7.2.*

D *See audio script 7.4.*

E

3 ✗   **4** ✓   **5** ✗

Survival business English

B *See audio script 7.7.*

D *See audio script 7.9.*

8 Planning

Sound work

B

/ɔː/	as in short course: **or**dinary
/uː/	as in school rules: d**o**
/ʌ/	as in much luck: **o**ther
/ɜː/	as in first term: w**or**k
/ə/	as in a'bout 'Can**a**da: inform**a**tion
/əʊ/	as in go slow: **o**verspend

C *See audio script 8.2.*

F *See audio script 8.5.*

Survival business English

A *See audio script 8.6.*

B *See audio script 8.7.*

C *See audio script 8.7.*

9 Managing people

Sound work

A *See audio script 9.1.*

C *See audio script 9.3.*

D *See audio script 9.4.*

Survival business English

A *See audio script 9.5.*

B *See audio script 9.6.*

C

1 b   **2** b   **3** a   **4** c   **5** c

D Sample answers

2 Sue Short from Datatrax phoned about your order number AB/987. She said they didn't have Item 14 in stock. She asked if they could send you another model of the same quality.
3 Phil from Human Resources phoned about next week's job interviews. He asked how many candidates you wanted to interview. He also asked if you needed any help.
4 Yeliz Gumus rang about your visit to Izmir. She said she'd booked you into the Crowne Plaza Hotel. She asked if you could send her your flight details.

10 Conflict

Sound work

B *See audio script 10.2.*

D *See audio script 10.4.*

E *See audio script 10.5.*

Survival business English

A

Speaker 1: e
Speaker 2: f
Speaker 3: a
Speaker 4: g
Speaker 5: b

B

Speaker 1: f
Speaker 2: g
Speaker 3: e
Speaker 4: b
Speaker 5: c

C *See audio script 10.7.*

11 New business

Sound work

B *See audio script 11.2.*

D *See audio script 11.4.*

F *See audio script 11.6.*

Survival business English

A *See audio script 11.7.*

B *See audio script 11.8.*

C *See audio script 11.9.*

E *See audio script 11.11.*

12 Products

Sound work

A *See audio script 12.1.*

B

2 It has
3 Its
4 Its / it is
5 It has
6 It is

C

1 It's (It is) delivered
2 They're (They are) manufactured
3 It was modified
4 They were discontinued
5 It's (It has) been advertised
6 They've (They have) been promoted
7 It'll (It will) be tested
8 They'll (They will) be insured

D

c 5   **d** 6   **e** 4   **f** 2   **g** 7   **h** 1

Survival business English

A

1 c   **2** a   **3** b   **4** b   **5** c   **6** a

B *See audio script 12.6.*

C

a 5   **b** 1   **c** 6   **d** 3   **e** 2   **f** 4

Audio scripts

Introduction

The sounds of English

Vowel sounds

/ɪ/	quick fix	/ɔ:/	short course
/i:/	clean sheet	/ʊ/	good books
/e/	sell well	/u:/	school rules
/æ/	bad bank	/ʌ/	much luck
/ɑ:/	smart card	/ɜ:/	first term
/ɒ/	top job	/ə/	a'bout 'Canada

Diphthongs

/eɪ/	play safe	/əʊ/	go slow
/aɪ/	my price	/ɪə/	near here
/ɔɪ/	choice oil	/eə/	fair share
/aʊ/	downtown	/ʊə/	tour

Consonants
1 Contrasting voiceless and voiced consonants

Voiceless		Voiced	
/p/	pay	/b/	buy
/f/	file	/v/	value
/t/	tax	/d/	deal
/θ/	think	/ð/	this
/tʃ/	cheap	/dʒ/	job
/s/	sell	/z/	zero
/k/	card	/g/	gain
/ʃ/	option	/ʒ/	decision

2 Other consonants

/m/	mine	/n/	net
/ŋ/	branding	/h/	high
/l/	loss	/r/	rise
/w/	win	/j/	year

1 Careers

1.1
Tim; team   pick; peak   bit; beat

1.2
/ɪ/ as in quick fix: manager; mechanic; editor
/i:/ as in clean sheet: teacher; policeman; art dealer

1.3
She can speak Arabic.
She can't speak Greek.
She can speak Arabic, but she can't speak Greek.

1.4
1 He can use Visual Basic, but he can't use Java.
2 She can't start this week, but she can start by the end of the month.
3 I can't speak Mandarin fluently, but I can understand a lot.
4 We can let you know next week, but we can't promise anything.
5 She can use spreadsheets, but she can't design a website.

1.5
1 Can you hold?
2 Did you say R-E-I-T-H?
3 Hello. Is that John Reith?
4 Could you take a message?
5 Could you tell me your name and address?

1.6
1 Can I have your name?
2 Just one moment, please.
3 Hold on.
4 I'd like to speak to Ms Allan.
5 I'm afraid she's in a meeting just now.
6 Can I take a message?
7 Could you ask her to call me back this afternoon?

1.7
/eɪ/   as in play safe: a; h; j; k
/i:/   as in clean sheet: b; c; d; e; g; p; t; v
/e/   as in sell well: f; l; m; n; s; x; z
/aɪ/   as in my price: i; y
/əʊ/ as in go slow: o
/u:/   as in school rules: q; u; w
/ɑ:/   as in smart card: r

1.8
1 Hello. My name's Glen Strachan. That's S-T-R-A-C-H-A-N.
2 The address is 47, Buccleuch Square, Edinburgh. I'll spell that for you: B-U-C-C-L-E-U-C-H.
3 So I'll go over the name of the street again: El Falaky. That's E-L, new word, F-A-L-A-K-Y, number 52, Cairo.
4 I work for de Vuyst Consultants in Brussels, that's small D-E new word V-U-Y-S-T. Got that?
5 Miyako? Sure. M-I-Y-A-K-O.

1.9
1 00 386 61 24661 87
2 00 90 212 613 3367

1.10
1 If you'd like more details, please call our Bucharest office on 00 40 1 3322 040.
2 And our number in Tunis is 216 1 768 009.
3 Please contact our Montevideo subsidiary. The country code is 598, and their number is 2 600 5467.
4 Yes, we do have an office in Madrid. The number is 328 67 53. The country code is 34, by the way, and then 91 for Madrid.
5 Our agent in Bratislava can be reached on 421 7 753 0886.

2 Selling online

2.1
1 ret**ai**ler; **pay**ment; exch**a**nged
2 ref**u**nd; disc**ou**nt; **o**ffer
3 meth**o**d; **o**ffer; st**o**ck
4 ret**u**rn; **se**rvice; **pur**chase
5 gr**o**ceries; cl**o**thes; neg**o**tiate
6 desp**a**tch; s**a**les; exch**a**nge

2.2
1 Online retailers have to offer secure guarantees to the public.
2 We have to order some photocopying paper.
3 Their site is easy to visit. You don't have to register.
4 You'll have to pay on receipt of the goods.
5 They'll have to redesign their website.

2.3
1 If we want them to finish this month, they'll have to work weekends.
2 If they have to work weekends, they'll need to be paid overtime.
3 If they're paid overtime, our production costs will increase.
4 If our production costs increase, we may have to raise our prices.
5 If we raise our prices again, no one knows what will happen.

2.4
1 A: Right. Let's get started, shall we? If we buy 100 'Hit' and 200 'Tournament' tennis rackets, what discount can you offer us?
2 B: On an order of that size, and since it's your first order with us, we can offer 5%. But then we can offer 10% off all quoted prices for further orders above 6,000 euros.
3 A: All right, that sounds reasonable. Now, if we place an order this week, will you be able to deliver the goods within two weeks?
4 B: Certainly. And as regards payment, we would expect you to pay by bank transfer as soon as the goods have been shipped.
5 A: Well, we'd rather pay by letter of credit.
6 B: Mmm, let me think about that. If we agree to let you pay by letter of credit, then you'll have to pay within 30 days, and you'll have to be responsible for insurance as well.
7 A: Fine. That's it, then. I think we've covered everything.

2.5
1 A: If we order 200 units, will you give us a 10% discount?
  B: I'm afraid we can only offer 5% on orders of that size.
2 C: We would expect you to cover insurance as well.
  D: Sorry, but we can't agree to that. We can only cover freight.
3 A: We'd like you to deliver immediately.
  B: I'm sorry, but that's not acceptable. We can just guarantee delivery within ten days.
4 A: We'll ship the goods by train. Is that all right?
  B: We'd rather you shipped them by road, in fact.
5 C: You'll have to pay us in advance this time.
  D: Well, we'd prefer to pay you on delivery as usual.

3 Companies

3.1
1 syllable: deals; makes
2 syllables: involves; recruits
3 syllables: finances; develops

3.2
1 raises   5 improves
2 starts   6 increases
3 employs   7 costs
4 delivers   8 produces

3.3
1 finances   3 increases
2 raises   4 produces

3.4
1 We need people who are reliable.
2 The chocolates are made in Turin.
3 Our new products are not selling well.

3.5
1 We're making good progress.
2 We make luxury chocolates.
3 They do a lot of business with India.
4 They're doing quite well this year.
5 We develop ten new products every year.
6 We're developing a new computer system.

3.6
Zengő Furniture Company Rt. (ZFC Rt.) specialises in manufacturing and retailing office furniture. Based in Pécsvárad, in the south of Hungary, we are the leading Hungarian company in our field. We operate eight stores located throughout the country and employ 145 people altogether.
Last year our sales rose to over 40 million euros, which represents a 19% increase over the previous year. Our earnings before interest and tax were 4.9 million euros, or 12% of sales. This result is better than the result we achieved the year before, when the margin was equal to 8.7% of sales.

3.7
I = Interviewer, P = Pierre
I: So, Mr Chevrel, your company is called *Espace Mode*. Is that how you say it?
P: That's right, yes. Exactly.
I: Where are you based, and what exactly do you do?
P: We are situated in Grenoble, and we are manufacturers and retailers of clothes under the 'C-Kool' and 'Mirabelle' brand names.
I: Who are your customers?
P: Young men and women from all walks of life, in the age range 16–25. People who want to feel good and look beautiful! And we also supply wholesale products to agents and mail order catalogues.
I: What's the current position of your company? And how many people do you employ?
P: Well, we are among the French top three in the clothing sector. And as regards our workforce, we employ almost 300 people.
I: Now that we are on to figures, would you like to give us some financial information?

P: Certainly. Last year, we achieved an annual turnover of over 190 million euros and generated profits of 7.6 million, that is to say 4% of sales.

I: Finally, how about the future?

P: We're working on exciting new designs which will reflect a completely new concept of teenage fashion. I'm sure this will make *Espace Mode* the leader of the European fashion market.

I: We are certainly looking forward to seeing those new designs. Thank you very much, Mr Chevrel. We now come to the end of our business programme …

4 Great ideas

4.1
1 started; decided
2 developed; introduced
3 exploited; discussed
4 received; launched
5 used; changed
6 finished; stopped

4.2
1 **syllable:** moved; asked; touched
2 **syllables:** prepared: reduced: wanted
3 **syllables:** attracted: discovered; established

4.3
1 preferred
2 helped
3 financed
4 adapted
5 offered
6 earned
7 worked
8 advertised

4.4
1 A: Were they trying to develop a new drug?
   B: Well, everybody thinks they were.
2 A: She was travelling around the world on her own.
   B: Are you sure she was?
3 A: Our competitors weren't promoting their range of products very well.
   B: Weren't they really?
4 A: The new product wasn't attracting a lot of customers.
   B: Well, in fact I think it was.
5 A: He was planning the next advertising campaign.
   B: Yeah, and he was designing a new product at the same time.

4.5
Speaker 1:
All right, then. It seems that we all agree when we should launch our new product, so let's move on now to advertising.

Speaker 2:
As you all know, the purpose of our meeting this afternoon is to decide how we're going to promote our new range.

Speaker 3:
It's getting rather late, so let's sum up and see what we've got so far.

Speaker 4:
Martin suggested that we should target supermarkets only. How do you feel about this? … Helen?

Speaker 5:
OK everyone? So, our next item on the agenda is our R&D budget.

Speaker 6:
Right. Quite a few suggestions have been made. So let's stop here for a minute and recap.

Speaker 7:
So, you know what the problem is, and you've heard a number of possible solutions. … What are your views on this? … Kim?

Speaker 8:
I've called this meeting to exchange ideas about a new marketing strategy.

4.6
1 Right. Let's now have a look at our sales figures.
2 I'm not very happy about that, I'm afraid.
3 Just a minute, please.
4 Shall we get started?
5 Let's get down to business.
6 Well, I'm not sure about that.
7 What exactly do you mean by 'specialist stores'?
8 I'm in favour of launching the product just before summer.

4.7
Shall we begin? As you know, we're going to launch a major new product – a unique soft drink with low sugar and carbon dioxide content. I've called this meeting for two main reasons. Firstly, we still have to agree when exactly we should launch the product. Secondly, we need your ideas for a new name, as many of you are not satisfied with the name *Vitafruit*. So, let's turn to the launch date. Sania, what do you think would be the best date?

5 Stress

5.1
1 pressure; problem; promotion
2 workload; lifestyle; deadline
3 contracts; asks; psychologists
4 He resigned three months ago.
5 It's a study about stress in the workplace.
6 She's planned lots of projects.

5.2
1 She's completely changed her lifestyle.
2 He hasn't seen a stress counsellor yet.
3 They've appointed a new management team.
4 They haven't introduced flexitime yet.

5.3
1 They've never made a presentation.
2 He's never travelled abroad.
3 They've gone on a training course.
4 She's been under a lot of stress.
5 He hasn't taken time off work this year.
6 We haven't finished our report.

5.4
1 They were overworked, weren't they?
2 She's been under stress recently, hasn't she?
3 They weren't feeling relaxed, were they?
4 You haven't missed the deadline, have you?
5 He resigned last week, didn't he?
6 She didn't come to work yesterday, did she?

5.5
a) B: How about introducing flexitime?
b) B: We could make sure they don't have to work overtime more than once a week.
c) B: Well, I suggest you take it home with you and finish it over the weekend, then.
d) B: Shall we call a meeting to discuss the problem, so we can look for ways of making them less strict?
e) B: What about asking your boss to stop putting them up?
f) B: Well, I think we should make it absolutely clear to everyone that only mobiles may be used for private conversations.

5.6
1 C: What about finishing earlier on Fridays?
2 A: Why don't we have individual interviews with each member of staff?
3 D: Have you thought of making working hours more flexible?
4 B: I think we should forbid smoking on all our premises.
5 A: Why don't we redecorate the staff restaurant to make it look more cheerful?
6 B: How about offering staff free yoga classes?
7 D: I suggest that we increase staff holidays from three to four weeks.

6 Entertaining

6.1
change; programme; theatre; want; talk; starter

6.2
/ə/   as in a'bout 'Canada: company; corporate
/æ/   as in bad bank: access; thanks
/eɪ/   as in play safe: favourite; spacious
/ɔː/   as in short course: always; call
/ɑː/   as in smart card: large; target
/ɒ/   as in top job: watch; quality

6.3
1 She put off the meeting.
2 She put it off.
3 I looked up their address.
4 I looked it up.

6.4
1 Several extra visitors turned up.
2 They took up our invitation.
3 She took us out to an excellent restaurant.
4 We should set up online sales as soon as we can.

6.5
1 A: David, have you met Elisa Vasconcelos?
   B: No. Hello, Elisa. Nice to meet you.
2 A: Jameel, do you know Sylvia?
   B: Yes, of course. Hi Sylvia, good to see you again.
3 A: How do you do . My name's Joko Hartono.
   B: Nice to meet you. Mine's Brendan Lenehan.
4 A: How are things?
   B: Fine thanks. It's good to be here.
5 A: Can I get you something to drink?
   B: That would be nice. Thanks. I'll have some fruit juice.

6.6
1 Did your flight get in on time?
2 How's your hotel?
3 Have you been here before?
4 Do you know your way around?
5 How long are you staying?
6 Could I use your phone, please?

6.7
1 I've just got off the train from Kyiv.
2 The food here is really delicious.
3 My daughter plays the piano as well.
4 I go to tai chi classes three times a week.
5 I'm in food quality control.
6 I worked in Malaysia for three years.
7 I'm from Gdansk.

7 Marketing

7.1
/ɒ/   as in top job: loss; shop; what
/ɔː/   as in short course: launch; store; caught

7.2
/ɒ/   as in top job: model; product; quality; want
/ɔː/   as in short course: corporate; course; forecast

7.3
Which age group do you belong to?
How much did you spend on soft drinks last month?
Would you consider buying a different brand?

7.4
1 Do you take the packaging into account?
2 How often do you buy spring water?
3 How many bottles of water did you buy last week?
4 Would you try fruit-flavoured mineral water?
5 What kind of soft drinks do you usually buy?

7.5
1 product; order; service
2 credit; payment; success
3 campaign; forecast; figures
4 quality; packaging; marketing
5 customer; department; specialist

7.6

1 A: ... and your agent in Uruguay is Juan José Buaro. B-U-A-R-O ...

   B: Sorry, no. B-U-<u>E</u>-R-O.

2 A: All right. See you on Tuesday, then.

   B: Hold on a minute. The meeting is on <u>Thurs</u>day.

7.7

1 A: Ah, hello Miss Peterson.

   B: Hello Mr Gallegos, it's <u>Mrs</u> Peterson, actually. How can I help you?

2 A: ... and my sales report will be with you by the thirtieth.

   B: Sorry, Ranesh. We're talking about the thir<u>teen</u>th.

3 A: So their number is 020 8224 7895.

   B: No, 8224 <u>6</u>895.

4 A: ... and you said the advertising agency was at 75 Birchington Street.

   B: Well, it's Birchington <u>Road</u>, actually.

5 A: Good to hear you increased your market share by 9.5%.

   B: Sorry – I said <u>5</u>.5%.

6 A: I hear 40% of the people you interviewed had difficulty finding our products.

   B: That's not quite right, I'm afraid. I said <u>14</u>%.

7.8

1 A: We interviewed more than ***** people.

   B: Sorry, how many people did you interview?

2 A: ***** is unhappy about our sales figures.

   B: The line's very bad, I'm afraid. Who's unhappy about our sales figures?

7.9

1 A: So our new hair conditioner will be launched on *****.

   B: I couldn't hear you. When will it be launched?

2 A: We've already spent ***** on advertising.

   B: Sorry? How much have you spent?

3 A: The ***** Manager was really very pleased.

   B: Sorry, who was very pleased?

4 A: He'd like to meet you on ***** in the afternoon.

   B: It's a very bad line. When would he like to meet me?

5 A: Our new range of toiletries should be targeted at *****.

   B: Sorry? Who should our new range be targeted at?

6 A: Our total sales were over *****.

   B: Sorry, how much were they?

8 Planning

8.1

h**o**liday; d**o**; inf**or**mation; **or**dinary; **o**ther; **o**verspend; w**or**k

8.2

/ɒ/ as in t**o**p j**o**b: h**o**liday; **o**ffice

/ɔː/ as in sh**or**t c**our**se: **or**dinary; **for**ecast

/uː/ as in sch**oo**l r**u**les: d**o**; m**o**ve

/ʌ/ as in m**u**ch l**u**ck: **o**ther; c**o**mpany

/ɜː/ as in f**ir**st t**er**m: w**or**k; w**or**ld

/ə/ as in **a**'bout 'Can**a**d**a**: inf**or**mation; peri**o**d

/əʊ/ as in g**o** sl**ow**: **o**verspend; **o**pen

8.3

1 They expect to make a huge profit.

2 They're going to relaunch the series very soon.

3 They're hoping to attract foreign investors.

8.4

1 What are you going to do?

2 They intend to expand in Poland.

3 He's planning to take early retirement.

4 We're hoping to open a subsidiary in Madrid.

5 They're going to do some research on their new product.

8.5

1 in<u>form</u>; infor<u>ma</u>tion

2 <u>im</u>plement; implemen<u>ta</u>tion

3 pre<u>pare</u>; prepa<u>ra</u>tion

4 con<u>si</u>der; conside<u>ra</u>tion

5 <u>ce</u>lebrate; cele<u>bra</u>tion

6 <u>re</u>novate; reno<u>va</u>tion

7 ex<u>pand</u>; ex<u>pan</u>sion

8 ex<u>pect</u>; expec<u>ta</u>tion

9 <u>mo</u>dernise; moderni<u>sa</u>tion

10 dis<u>cuss</u>; dis<u>cu</u>ssion

11 de<u>cide</u>; de<u>ci</u>sion

12 re<u>vise</u>; re<u>vi</u>sion

8.6

1 A: We forecast an increase in sales.

   B: Are you saying that business is picking up, then?

2 A: I don't think I can finish my report by Wednesday.

   B: So what you're saying is that you won't be able to meet the deadline.

3 A: Unfortunately, they did not estimate the costs properly.

   B: You mean, it was a lot more expensive?

4 A: I hope Peterson will attend the board meeting.

   B: You mean, you're not completely sure he'll come?

5 A: They're not expecting to move into their new offices until January.

   B: So what you're saying is that they are not sticking to their plan.

6 A: It seems that there's going to be a slight delay.

   B: What exactly do you mean by 'slight delay'?

8.7

Kati: Ana?

Ana: Yes. Speaking.

Kati: Hi. I'm phoning about our visitors from Stockholm. I'm afraid they've changed their plans.

Ana: You mean, they<u>'re not coming</u> next week?

Kati: Yes, they are. But they<u>'re arriving</u> on Thursday, not on Wednesday as they originally planned.

Ana: I see. So what about our meeting?

Kati: Well, I think they<u>'re going to be</u> very busy all day Thursday. You know, the Performance Evaluations and all that. They could see you after that, but I'm sure Friday morning would be better. Would 10 o'clock be convenient for you?

Ana: Well, I<u>'m seeing</u> an important client at 10.15. I can't change that, I'm afraid.

Kati: How about earlier, say 8.30?

Ana: All right. Let's make it 8 o'clock, just to be on the safe side.

Kati: Fine. I<u>'ll confirm</u> the appointment as soon as possible.

Ana: Thanks, Kati. That's great.

9 Managing people

9.1
1 sales; training; persuasive; pay
2 launch; order; report; talk
3 money; number; other; trust
4 flow; approach; goal; shareholder

9.2
1 They told every one of us.
2 She finds it easy to delegate authority.
3 He believes in his employees' abilities.
4 They've invested a lot in training courses.
5 She likes to communicate information as often as possible.

9.3
1 He gained a lot of experience abroad.
2 She told us that Alan wouldn't agree.
3 The department isn't investing enough in training.

9.4
budget; invoice
mistake; support
shareholder; deputy; manager
suggestion; assistant; consultant

9.5
1 Keep in touch.
2 We'll be in touch soon.
3 Have a safe journey back.
4 I hope we'll see you again soon.
5 Thanks for looking after me so well.
6 Thanks ever so much for your hospitality.

9.6
1 A: What do you usually do after work?
    B: Not much. I sometimes watch a video.
2 A: Any plans for this evening?
    B: Well, I'd just like to stay in the hotel and relax.
3 A: What do people here usually do at weekends?
    B: Many people go to their holiday cottages in the hills.
4 A: We're going out. Why don't you join us?
    B: That's very kind of you, but some other time.
5 A: How do you usually spend the summer?
    B: We all go to see my parents in Toulouse.
6 A: So what do you think of Copenhagen?
    B: It's great. Thanks for showing me around.

9.7
1 We're all sorry to see you leave.
2 It's been a pleasure working with you.
3 Goodbye. All the best.
4 Thanks very much for your hospitality.
5 Have a good weekend.

9.8
1 Hello. This is Max. I'm calling about your presentation on Friday. Just a couple of questions. What time would you like to start? And is the board room OK? Thanks. Bye.
2 Hi. Sue Short from Datatrax here. I'm phoning about your order number AB/987. We don't have Item 14 in stock, I'm afraid. Can we send you another model of the same quality?

3 Hi. This is Phil from Human Resources. I'm phoning about next week's job interviews. How many candidates do you want to interview? And something else: do you need any help?
4 Hello. Yeliz Gumus here. I'm ringing about your visit to Izmir. I've booked you into the Crowne Plaza Hotel. Could you send me your flight details, by the way? Thanks.

10 Conflict

10.1
patient; nervous
propose; success
behaviour; consistent
compromise; sympathy

10.2
advice; solution; company; complaint; customer; entertainment

10.3
We won't pay.
We'll see.
We wouldn't answer.
We'd complain.
I'll do it.
I'd agree.
She'll send it.
She'd sign it.

10.4
1 I'd resign immediately.
2 I'll send them a fax.
3 We'll deliver the goods this week.
4 They'd close our account.
5 We wouldn't reduce the price.
6 We'd pay all transport costs.
7 They won't pay you a higher commission.
8 We won't sign the contract.

10.5
1 If we pay late, they'll close our account.
2 If you delivered this week, we'd pay all transport costs.
3 If you gave us a 10% discount, we'd place our order early next week.
4 If you exceed the sales target, they'll give you a bonus.
5 If you pay cash, we'll give you an extra discount.

10.6
Speaker 1:
... so it was relatively easy to agree on transport and insurance, but they wouldn't give us the usual 10% discount. We told them 5% was unacceptable. They wouldn't compromise, so in the end we said we didn't want the goods, and we turned to a new supplier.

Speaker 2:
... yeah, bosses come and go, don't they? The new one seems OK. At least she listens to us.
That's what we need in sales – more than in any other department, I think. The one before was so inconsistent and unsympathetic, he just couldn't work with us. That's when three of our best representatives decided to leave the company.

Speaker 3:
... and he called me into his office on Tuesday morning and started shouting at me! Would you believe it? He said that I always handed in my reports late. Fortunately, I still had that e-mail he'd sent me, informing me he was expecting my report on Thursday afternoon. I showed it to him, and in the end he did say he was sorry for being unfair. Good thing he did, otherwise I was prepared to resign.

Speaker 4:
Every week I had four or five employees come up to me and complain about all the paperwork and about having to work much longer hours because of that. I knew they were right; there had been far too many redundancies. What could I do? I thought the best compromise was to hire some part-time administrative assistants, and that's exactly what we did.

Speaker 5:
We were working on the same project in three different teams, each working according to a different schedule. We were getting on well in my team – until Tony Debeer joined us, that is. We disagreed about almost everything, and I found him very arrogant. We couldn't be more different, in fact. I found it all very stressful, so I just said to our team leader that the schedule no longer suited me, and I asked her to transfer me to another team.

10.7
A: Phillip's Office Supplies International. Good morning.
B: It's Mary Li here, from Sun Sing Advertising.
A: Hello, Ms Li. How can I help you?
B: I'd like to make a complaint.
A: What seems to be the trouble?
B: You have just sent us the wrong invoice, I'm afraid.
A: Can you give me the details, please?
B: Right. The invoice number is 202.A and the order number you quote is BG/505. In fact, our order number is BG/503.
A: Now, let me see ... I'm terribly sorry. It's our fault entirely. I'm afraid there's been a mix-up.
B: When do you think you can sort it out?
A: I'll look into it and call you back as soon as possible.
B: Thank you.
A: Don't mention it. Goodbye, Ms Li.

11 New business

11.1
n**o**t; n**ough**t   sp**o**t; sp**or**t   sh**o**t; sh**or**t

11.2
1 We'll send them <u>a</u>ll on a training c<u>our</u>se.
2 Let's s<u>or</u>t out this problem bef<u>ore</u> Pauline gets here.
3 Acc<u>or</u>ding to this rep<u>or</u>t, interest rates will soon f<u>a</u>ll.
4 We need to ref<u>or</u>m our tax system in <u>or</u>der to stimulate exp<u>or</u>ts.
5 They've closed 40 of their st<u>or</u>es and cut their workf<u>or</u>ce by a qu<u>ar</u>ter.

11.3
1 As soon‿as‿interest rates fall, consumer spending goes‿up.
2 I'll sign the new contract‿as soon‿as‿I've read‿all the details.

11.4
1 We'll set‿up‿in that‿area when the situation has‿improved.
2 We'll sort‿it‿out when‿Allan‿arrives.

11.5
1 January the twentieth   2 the twelfth of October

11.6
1 the <u>four</u>teenth of <u>February</u>   4 De<u>cember</u> the seven<u>teenth</u>
2 Sep<u>tember</u> the fif<u>teenth</u>   5 the <u>third</u> of <u>June</u>
3 the <u>six</u>teenth of <u>April</u>   6 the <u>fourth</u> of <u>July</u>

11.7
1 Thirteen pounds
2 Forty percent
3 Three hundred and fifty million
4 One thousand four hundred and sixteen yen
5 Eighty thousand dollars
6 One thousand two hundred euros
7 Two-fifths

11.8
1 A: Did the unemployment rate decrease?
   B: Yes. It went down by 0.5% to reach 11.3%.
2 A: Do you know the Footsie index?
   B: Hold on ... Yes. It closed 114.2 points higher at 5,833.9 points.
3 A: What's the basic rate of income tax in the UK?
   B: Well, it was reduced from 23 to 22% a couple of years ago.
4 A: And what percentage of all income taxpayers pay the basic rate?
   B: About 75 or 80%, I think.
5 A: What's the euro – dollar exchange rate?
   B: Mmm, somewhere between 0.79 and 0.82 against the dollar, I'd say.
6 A: What's the population of the UK?
   B: Just over 60.5 million. So that's about 250 people per square kilometer.

11.9
And now in our business programme, here is *The Country in Figures*.
The growth rate of the economy last year was 3.1%, and the GDP per capita was $26,200.
The inflation rate was 2.3%.
The labour force is estimated at 2.967 million; 81% are employed in the services, 14% in industry, and 5% in agriculture.
The unemployment rate fell to 4.9%.
Finally, let's turn to the budget. Revenues totalled $54.7 billion, and expenditure $53.1 billion.
With me in the studio is Professor Gary Myers of the National Institute of Economics. So, Professor Myers what are the prospects for the next six months?

11.10
1 A: Was that 2.5%?
   B: No. 2.<u>8</u>%.
2 A: Did you say 2.4%?
   B: Sorry, no. <u>3</u>.4%.

11.11
1 A: So the unemployment rate went up by 1.2%.
  B: Sorry, no, I said 1.1%.
2 A: So, 36.7% of the people in Denmark own a computer.
  B: 37.7%, to be precise.
3 A: Did you say the GDP totalled £853 billion last year?
  B: Not quite. It was £843 billion.

12 Products

12.1
1 stylish; grow; produce
2 comfortable; manufacture
3 Our new products are attractive and practical.
4 They're also flexible and user-friendly.
5 We have a lot of products for customers with busy lifestyles.
6 They haven't announced the launch date yet.

12.2
1 It's ideal for storing CDs.
2 It's got lots of interesting features.
3 Its weight is just under 3 kilos.
4 Its most attractive feature is that it's easy to operate.
5 It's got all you need for home and office use.
6 It's available in three different colours.

12.3
1 It's delivered
2 They're manufactured
3 It was modified
4 They were discontinued
5 It's been advertised
6 They've been promoted
7 It'll be tested
8 They'll be insured

12.4
a) It was modified after the tests.
b) They'll be insured against fire.
c) It's been advertised in all national newspapers.
d) They've been promoted to senior managers.
e) They were discontinued because of poor sales.
f) They're manufactured in Korea.
g) It'll be tested in our laboratories.
h) It's delivered within a week.

12.5
1 Could you tell us something about the special features of your office furniture?
2 What colours is it available in?
3 And what about the weight of this handheld TV?
4 Did you say it has an energy-saving device?
5 So, what's its unique selling point?
6 What kind of guarantee do you offer?

12.6
Our new model has several special features which will appeal to our customers. It's stylish, and it's made of stainless steel. It weighs just under 2.2 kilos, and its length is 21 centimeters. It's ideal for the office. Another advantage is that it's very user friendly. And finally, it costs 99 euros. Great value for money.

12.7
1 ... and it comes in two elegant colours and gives you optimum efficiency while taking up a minimum of space. In just a few minutes water is heated to the ideal temperature for a rich Italian taste. And a small heater built into the top will always keep your cups perfectly warm ...
2 ... and it's got a timer, which makes it ideal for office or domestic use. It's 75cm high, 45cm wide, and 30cm deep, and weighs 40kg. It's ideal for room sizes of up to 25 sq m. Besides its incredible cooling facility, it also has a heating mode ...
3 ... it is designed for those who want hi-tech in their business and need high-quality colour documents. It can detect paper type, and then select the ideal mode for any paper and film ...
4 ... it is the most exclusive model in our Eternity collection, designed for you to enjoy the art of precision timekeeping. It has got a steel casing, a pearl white dial, and a large red second hand. It comes with a black natural rubber strap that has our logo in blue and white enamel on it ...
5 ... it is robust, but not noticed easily. It uses PIR (Passive Infra Red technology) to detect body heat if somebody breaks in. And the whole system is controlled by a user-friendly keypad ...
6 ... Spacious and light, it is provided with a removable divider, key operated locks and digital combination. Made from highly resistant cowhide leather, it includes a new innovative twisting handle ...